Contents

Foreword - Sir Richard Knowles v

Preface to the First Edition vii

Preface to the Third Edition viii

Acknowledgements viii

1. **Heart of the City** 1

2. **Earlier Times** 15

3. **Boulton, Watt and Soho** 31

4. **Canals Rediscovered** 45

5. **An Urban Jewel** 65

6. **Victorian and Modern** 83

7. **Art on the Streets** 107

8. **City of Culture** 127

9. **Industry & Commerce** 143

10. **Life in the City** 163

Bibliography 181

Index 182

Page numbers for photographs are shown in bold in the index.

Positively Birmingham

Jonathan Berg

Birmingham Picture Library

First Published in 1994 by
Birmingham Picture Library
14 St Bernard's Road, Olton, Solihull, B92 7BB
Tel: 0121-765-4114 Fax: 0121-765-4224

Second edition 1997
Third edition 1999

ISBN 0 9523179 6 6

British Library Cataloguing in Publication Data
A catalogue record for this book is available from the British
Library.

An official millennium book of Birmingham

Design and Typesetting by John Williams,
Piggott Printers Limited, Cambridge.

Printed by Piggott Printers Limited, Cambridge.

Foreword

Some five years ago, when I was the Lord Mayor of Birmingham, I wrote the foreword to the first edition of *Positively Birmingham*. At that time I said that it was a book of stature, a book that any proud Birmingham man or woman could give to friends or firms could give to valued customers. That is even truer of this third edition. Now, with the first and second editions sold out Jonathan has completely updated the text and included over 100 new photographs. This new edition is being promoted as 'an official millennium book of Birmingham' with the blessing of the City Council.

Birmingham is no longer the grim industrial city which the folk memory of those of us born south of the River Thames carried with us, nor indeed is it thought of as the 'workshop of the world' anymore. The National Exhibition Centre and the International Convention Centre have changed that image and there is more business tourism here than any other city outside London. However, we must not forget that this is still a city of industry, with a wealth of engineering expertise and a growing interest in the new technologies. Co-operation between the City Council, the Birmingham Chamber of Commerce and Industry and the business world has shown just how much can be achieved with a partnership approach.

Sir Richard Knowles

The city is alive at night with three great theatres, jazz concerts, early English music, the finest Symphony Hall in Europe and the National Indoor Arena. At night Broad Street and Brindleyplace are a hive of activity in the best tradition of great European cities. This is persuading many more people to live in the city centre again where the canal frontages can be attractive and quiet places rather than the 'dirty ditches' of old.

Our city is multi-racial with twenty-five percent of our people having a background that is Black or Asian and this adds variety and life for the enjoyment of everyone. We have learnt to live together and to appreciate the variety of music, dance and food which a multi-cultural society brings.

Positively Birmingham encapsulates all of this and makes it clear that a stay in Birmingham is a rewarding experience. This is not a coffee table book, but one that is meant to be picked up and read. It is an excellent background to a city that was described at the end of the nineteenth century as being 'the best governed city in the world'. Now, as we enter the twenty-first century, Birmingham is a good place in which to live. I am sure that this third edition will be as popular as the first two and I commend it to everybody.

Sir Richard Knowles
Citizen of Birmingham

July 1999

Preface to the First Edition

In 1990 I began to fulfil a long-standing ambition, by starting work on a book of photography of contemporary Birmingham. It was more luck than judgement that this coincided with such a dynamic time in the development of the city. Some major civic projects have now been completed, and this is an excellent time to reflect on the results of all this activity.

This book, then, contains the images of one Birmingham photographer. It is about things that have caught my imagination, and prompted me to explore further in today's city. The text aims to set the photographs in context, adding my personal feelings for this place.

For those interested in the technical side, most of the photographs were taken using a Bronica ETRS medium format camera. For architectural shots a Gandolfi 4" x 5" camera was used.

Birmingham is a complex city with an enormous number of different facets and it has been interesting for me to learn more about it as this book has developed, but of course there are many aspects not covered here. I hope that *Positively Birmingham* will give a feel for what I find a great city in which to live and work.

Jonathan Berg

July 1994

Preface to the Third Edition

The pace of change in Birmingham is evident for all to see. For this edition over half the photos are new and much additional material has been added. I have been photographing the city for ten years now and this book is a distillation of that work.

My approach has been to become increasingly inquisitive with my camera. This book demonstrates how much the city has achieved in recent years. For future generations *Positively Birmingham* will give a feel for Birmingham life and aspirations at the close of the twentieth-century and of this I am very proud.

Jonathan Berg

August 1999

Acknowledgements

Emphasis on photo-investigation has meant that many people have allowed me to enter their environment and I thank them all. Work was able to start on this book earlier than anticipated due to the International Congress of Actuaries giving 1,000 copies to their delegates. I am grateful to them and many other organisations that use the book as a gift, as only with such use is the book financially viable.

Sylvia Platt acted as editor and Rosanna Penn undertook additional proof-reading. I am grateful to Phil Roocroft, Nicola Poultney and Mike Taylor from Birmingham City Council and Sam Warnock, Joe McConnell and Philip Calcutt of Birmingham Marketing Partnership for advice. I appreciate the friendship and professionalism of John Williams, Mike Cartwright and all the staff at Piggott Printers.

JDB, August 1999

▶

Victoria Square Opening.
The official opening of Victoria Square by the Princess of Wales on 6 May 1993.

Chapter One

Heart of the City

Victoria Square demonstrates just how much is being achieved in Birmingham and is a good place to start this visual exploration of the city. It is a modern square and brings together Victorian buildings and modern public art on a large scale. It creates an interesting space in which to relax and has also become a focus for civic events.

Restoration of the Square was completed in 1993 and only then was our Victorian ancestors' dream of this place as a grand civic space fully realised. With the development of the city centre along Broad Street, Victoria Square is much more of a focal point, central to the pedestrian routes through the revitalised heart of Birmingham.

The Council House

The Council House is closely linked to Joseph Chamberlain and to the great municipal changes of the late nineteenth century. As Mayor of Birmingham, Chamberlain laid the foundation stone to the Council House on 14 June 1874, an event celebrated with a luncheon and fireworks in Aston Park. Yeoville Thomason, who had previously designed buildings in Colmore Row, won the competition for the Council House design amid much controversy and recrimination among the members of the council. The main façade has a mosaic by Salviati and sculptures including *Britannia Rewarding the Manufacturers of Birmingham* in the middle. The open space created in front was first known as Council House Square but when a statue of Queen Victoria was installed in 1901 it was renamed Victoria Square.

The Head Post Office, a Turning Point

Redevelopment of Birmingham City Centre in the 1960s and 1970s saw some fine Victorian buildings demolished to make way for the new civic buildings and the inner ring road. Campaigns were launched by the Victorian Society to try to save a number of buildings, successful in

The River (Dhruva Mistry, 1993) is the focal point of Victoria Square.

▶

2

the case of the French Renaissance-style Head Post Office in Victoria Square. This has been redeveloped (completed in 1991) and is now a high quality office block offering a modern environment in an historic setting. In 1973 permission had been granted to demolish the building and it was only vigorous campaigning by the Victorian Society members which saved this historic

The Head Post Office which dates from 1891. In the 1970s the Victorian Society mounted a successful campaign to stop the demolition of this building.

▼

Centrally placed on the façade
of the Council House is the
sculptural relief, Britannia
Rewarding the Manufacturers
of Birmingham (Lockwood,
Boulton and Sons).

building. This proved to be a turning point in
Victorian conservation in Birmingham. Adjacent to
the Post Office, Number 1 Victoria Square is a
modern office development, completed in 1985 on
the site of the old Parcels Office, and fortunately,
after further pressure from conservationists,
modified at the planning stage to ensure that it
was in keeping with surrounding buildings.

Classical Designs

The impressive Town Hall was designed by the
architects Hansom and Welch, who won the
architectural competition for its design in 1832.
Joseph Hansom is perhaps better remembered for
the Hansom Cab. The project was beset with
financial problems, ending with bankruptcy for
the architects and with the Birmingham architect
Edge completing the work. Although opened in
1834, the Town Hall was not finally complete until
1850. Constructed from Anglesey marble in a
classical design based on the temple of Castor and

Pollux in the Forum in Rome, it towered above the surroundings and influenced the design of the Victorian buildings which were to follow.

The Town Hall has played a part in some important historical events. The Chartist Movement, which promoted Parliamentary reform, was very powerful in the city, split between those favouring peaceful reform and those prepared to consider violent demonstrations. When Chartist riots broke out in 1839, the Town Hall was used as the headquarters for a two-thousand-strong special constabulary brought in to quell the uprising.

In 1901 at a meeting on the Boer War in the Town Hall, David Lloyd George, then a young Liberal MP, was prevented from speaking by a mob who gathered outside and began breaking windows. He is said to have escaped by borrowing a policeman's uniform and marching out of the hall as part of a police squad.

The Town Hall is a major component of Birmingham's architectural landscape. However, with the opening of Symphony Hall, the Town Hall's traditional role has been superseded and it was closed to the public in 1996. In 1999 a petition signed by 10,000 people demanded something should be done with the building which was starting to deteriorate. Plans that aim to convert the building back to a more flexible use are being considered and a music venue of this size and atmosphere is certainly needed in the city.

The Re-Making of Victoria Square

In the early 1990s major transformation of the city centre was undertaken. A pedestrianisation scheme with Victoria Square as the focal point now incorporates the space defined by the Town Hall, Council House, former Head Post Office and top of New Street. The nineteenth-century buildings around Victoria Square are in marked contrast to the twentieth-century backdrop to Centenary Square, which was completed just as plans for

Victoria Square became a reality. The statue of Queen Victoria and other important architectural and artistic features of the Square, notably the Council House, have been renovated and restored using the original stone.

Victoria Square Sculptures

Contemporary pieces of sculpture in the Square by Dhruva Mistry are sympathetic to their surroundings with their use of the traditional materials water, stone and bronze. Born in 1957 and brought up in India, Mistry studied sculpture at the University of Baroda and the Royal College

One of the two Guardians *(Dhruva Mistry, 1993) found either side of The River in Victoria Square.*
▼

of Art, had a residency at Kettle's Yard, Cambridge and is a Royal Academian. He explains his work as follows:

> The central feature of The River, *a monumental bronze fountain figure, is a metaphor for life source. It sits in a sandstone shell upheld by a group of encircling salmon. Eleven radiating water-jets punctuate the overflow of water from the shell into the upper pool.*

> *White-water springs forth from the hands of the River and cascades down the weir into the lower pool fountain of the* Youth. *The honeysuckle shaped fountain appears to float in the middle of the pool surrounded by four basic shapes on the floor; a cube, cone, cylinder and sphere. A boy and girl sit on the cube and cylinder respectively in a mood of quiet reflection.*

> The Victoria Square Guardians *are two large sphinx-like images as composite creatures, carved from Darley Dale sandstone, and which look over the lower pool piazza. These sculptures are symbolic protectors of the peace, pride and dignity of the square.*

> The Object-Variations, *a pair of sandstone lamp posts, flank the river to create a spatial relationship of the works, in and around the water feature, as upholders of light for the entire installation.*

▲

Setting the jets on The River *in April 1993.*

The Iron Man

Outside the old Head Post Office in Victoria Square is a cast-iron figure, twenty feet high, buried up to its calves and tilted at an angle. The ambiguity of this sculpture by Antony Gormley, now known as *Iron Man*, invites speculation by the viewer. The use of iron is a specific reference to Birmingham's industrial history. Like *Forward* in Centenary Square (page 113), *Iron Man* always arouses strong feelings. A proposal to run an extension of the Midland Metro up New Street and through Victoria Square is the biggest challenge yet for *Iron Man*. Antony Gormley followed *Iron Man* with the striking *Angel of the North* above the A1 at Gateshead which excites interest from all over the world and established his international reputation.

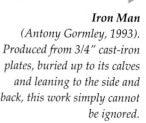

▶

Iron Man
(Antony Gormley, 1993).
Produced from 3/4" cast-iron plates, buried up to its calves and leaning to the side and back, this work simply cannot be ignored.

Birmingham on the World Stage

On 15 May 1998, after much planning and preparation, the G8 Summit came to Birmingham. This was a huge opportunity to put the city on the world stage. Preparations had been both innovative and extensive. A poster campaign encouraged Birmingham people to be proud of their city. One advert featured member of the public Marge Potter, and extolled her to "Get your hair done Marge, Bill Clinton's coming to town". Needless to say Marge looked immaculate as she went into the Council House reception and Bill, who needed some light relief at the time, told her that he had seen her poster in the White House.

The sun was out for the Summit weekend and the streets were awash with a mixture of activists and official and unofficial street entertainers. Pressure groups and demonstrators were keen to air their concerns. On G8 Saturday supporters of the Jubilee 2000 initiative, fighting to reduce world debt, arrived in the city from all over the country.

▲

Marge Potter, who featured in the G8 Summit advertising campaign, on her way to meet President Clinton.

Bill Clinton arrives in Victoria Square.

▼

After lunchtime picnics in city squares, demonstrators formed a human chain 50,000-strong to make their point.

Jubilee 2000 campaigned for the cancellation of loans to the world's poorest countries, where indebtedness spirals because of the inability to make basic interest payments. The campaigners clearly made an impression; debt relief was a central component of the G8 Summit conclusions.

▲

Tony and Cherie Blair meet local people and the media on the first day of the G8 Summit.

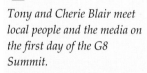

◄

Jubilee 2000 campaigners pressed their point on the cancellation of world debt for the world's poorest countries.

This weekend of worldwide publicity and promotion has had longer-term benefits for the city of Birmingham. This was the ultimate test of the infrastructure and expertise that had been developing around the National Exhibition Centre and International Convention Centre and everything worked out just fine. The Summit underlined the long-made claim of the city that it was a world-class meeting place.

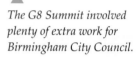

The G8 Summit involved plenty of extra work for Birmingham City Council.

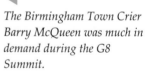

The Birmingham Town Crier Barry McQueen was much in demand during the G8 Summit.

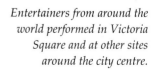

Entertainers from around the world performed in Victoria Square and at other sites around the city centre.

Lions on the Streets

In June 1998 Birmingham had only just recovered from the G8 Summit when over 25,000 International Lions from 185 different countries arrived for the largest convention the city had ever seen. The 81st International Lions Convention was only the second such event to be held in Europe. On day two of the five-day convention a five-hour parade, with 15,000 Lions parading in national costume, took place along Broad Street and surrounding streets.

Victoria Square has been transformed into the new focal point for the city and plays an important role in linking the commercial and shopping districts of the city with the redeveloped Broad Street and Centenary Square areas. In the dynamic Victorian era of Chamberlain's 'Municipal Revolution' in Birmingham the intention was to create a civic and cultural centre based on this square; now 130 years later these aspirations have finally been accomplished and with considerable style.

The International Lions took five hours to parade around the city as part of their convention.

St Nicholas's Church, King's Norton, *was rebuilt in the 14th century from an earlier Norman chapel. The south porch dates from the 15th century and parish business was often conducted here. Note the remains of the foliage dripstone round the arch. Just visible on the left-hand side, below the angel, are remains of a 'Mass' dial, which was a special sundial showing the time of the next mass.*

Chapter Two
Earlier Times

Reasons for the growth and development of Birmingham are complex and even learned historical texts are full of conjecture. Certainly Birmingham was not significant in Roman times - Metchley Camp, located on Birmingham University campus in Edgbaston, and the remains of a Roman road in Sutton Park are the only major relics from the Roman period. In the Domesday Book (1086) the manor of Birmingham was described as one of the poorest in the area.

A Marketplace

What gave rise to Birmingham's importance as a commercial and manufacturing centre? The city centre is built on a sandstone ridge between the rivers Tame and Rea. In the mid-twelfth century the hamlets around Birmingham needed a focus and in 1156 Peter de Bermingham, who controlled the Birmingham manor, seized an opportunity and was granted a market charter for the town; this encouraged early growth and development.

The close proximity to the Black Country, an area to the north-west of Birmingham which was rich in raw materials, was an important factor in the growth of industry in the town. Equally important were access to cheap energy - originally river

Birmingham University Field Archeology Unit undertook investigations at several sites as the Bull Ring Development commenced. At Edgbaston Street they found evidence in medieval remains that leather working had occurred as early as the 14th century, where previously it had been thought to date only from the 17th century.

By the middle of the 12th century the hamlets around Birmingham needed a trading centre. Birmingham took the initiative by obtaining a market charter from the Crown. To this day the Digbeth area of Birmingham is still very much a marketplace.

Birmingham as it is today.

▶

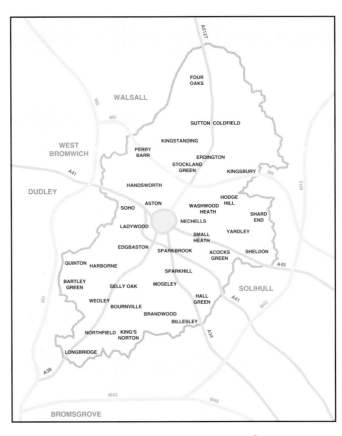

Birmingham city centre from Bordesley Village.
St Martin's Church is in the centre with the Bull Ring Centre just to the right. Other buildings that stand out include the Hyatt Hotel, Alpha Tower and the Rotunda.

▼

water to drive mills and later coal - the supply of cheap labour, a growing demand for household products and the town's entrepreneurial spirit. Surges in industrial production during periods of war have also promoted the growth of manufacturing over the centuries.

A Collection of Hamlets

In the thirteenth century there were some forty to fifty hamlets within today's city boundary and the

The Old Crown, Deritend.
Timber-framed and partly originating from 1368, this is thought to be the oldest building in the city centre. Close-by is the Custard Factory, formerly the home of Bird's Custard and now an arts and media centre.

remnants of life in these different parishes can be seen all over today's city - medieval churches in the Parishes of Sheldon, Aston, King's Norton and Yardley and half-timbered Grammar Schools at Yardley and King's Norton. Further examples of surviving ancient architecture include inns such as the Great Stone Inn at Northfield.

Half-Timbered Houses

During the reign of Henry VIII John Leland, a traveller, visited Birmingham. In 1538 he noted half-timbered houses and the parish church of St Martins, and saw that Birmingham was already involved in the metal trade, using iron and coal from the Black Country to produce items such as knives and nails in small forges and workshops. Buildings in the city centre from around this period include the Old Crown Inn in Digbeth High Street, and Stratford House at Camp Hill.

Surviving Old Buildings

The timber-framed Old Crown Inn, described by Leland as a 'mansion house of tymber', dates from

▲

Stratford House.
This is a superb building hidden away from the busy Stratford Road at Camp Hill. It was built in 1601 and restored in 1954.

◄

The Old Grammar School at Yardley.
Just one of many examples of the medieval past to be found in Birmingham's suburbs.

The Old Grammar School at King's Norton.
A medieval building dating from the 15th century. Originally it may have stood on stilts, the ground floor being added in the 16th century.

▼

1368 and is the oldest building in the centre of Birmingham. After being closed for some years the Old Crown was recently renovated and opened as a public house and restaurant.

Elizabethan and Jacobean buildings include Blakesley Hall at Yardley and, closer to the city centre, Stratford House at Camp Hill, originally built in 1601 as Ambrose Rotton's farm. From 1601 until the 1880s the house was in the ownership of just two families, the original Rottons and then the

St Nicholas's Church sits above the Canal House (1796) and junction of the Worcester and Birmingham and Stratford canals at King's Norton.

▶

Blakesley Hall is a yeoman's house dating from about 1550; it is open to the public and run by the Birmingham Museums and Art Gallery.

▶

Simcox family. During the second part of the nineteenth century, as Birmingham rapidly expanded, the house became surrounded by back-to-back housing. In 1926 Stratford House was sold to the LMS Railway who threatened to demolish it to make space for a goods yard. However, they gave way to public pressure and the building remains standing, having been renovated in 1954 by Ivon Adams, and it is now used as offices.

Aston Hall and Park

During the late sixteenth and early seventeenth centuries a substantial number of English country houses were built. The large number of new titles granted or, more accurately, sold by James I early in the seventeenth century contributed to this period of extravagant building styles. Aston Hall was one of the largest country houses built during this period in Warwickshire, and a demonstration of the Holte family's success.

Building commenced in 1618; the house was occupied in 1631 and Aston Hall completed in 1635. Good-quality building materials and design were used throughout. For example, instead of rubble foundations as was common at that time, the Hall sits on iron slag, most likely from a furnace at Aston. At a time when most houses in the area were timber-framed, bricks for the Hall were manufactured in temporary kilns set up in the Park.

James Watt Jnr.

In 1817 the Aston Hall estate was divided by Act of Parliament and the Hall, with some of the Park, was sold. From 1818 James Watt Jnr. rented Aston Hall. He ran the Soho Manufactory and Foundry with Matthew Robinson Boulton, son of the

The Long Gallery, Aston Hall, is 136 feet long and shows fine original decoration. Little has changed since pre-Victorian times.

◀

Aston Hall is a Jacobean
country house. The Park is
bordered by Aston Villa
football ground on one side
and the busy A38(M) on
the other.

The kitchen at Aston Hall was added in the mid-18th century. James Watt Jnr. installed a patent steam kitchen range.

famous Birmingham industrialist, Matthew Boulton. Aston Hall was the ideal home for Watt. It was close to Soho, appealed to his interest in antiquity and provided a very prestigious place to entertain guests. Indeed, in 1830 Princess Victoria dined at Aston Hall after a tour of the Soho factories. As a tenant, Watt made few structural changes, though he did install modern devices such as a steam kitchen range and hot-air heating.

Corporate Events

In 1848, after James Watt Jnr.'s death, Aston Hall was left empty and in 1850 it was offered for sale to the Corporation of Birmingham. However, negotiations broke down and a group of country gentlemen and artisans formed The Aston Hall and Park Company with the intention of purchasing it. Queen Victoria helped by returning to open

Visitors can get some hands-on experience at Aston Hall at special events during summer months.

the house and an exhibition of Birmingham industrial products on 15 June 1858. Literary dinners and 'old-time Christmas revels' were held to try and raise the additional funds for the purchase; the park was even hired out for corporate celebrations. It was at one such event that Selena Powell, an acrobat known as 'The Female Blondin' fell to her death from a tightrope. After this, Queen Victoria wrote to the town council expressing her displeasure that the park was being used for purposes other than healthy exercise and recreation. Even before this episode the Aston Hall and Park Company was in serious financial difficulty. In November 1863 Queen Victoria wrote again suggesting that a town with such wealth should be able to find the funds to purchase Aston Hall for the population. Finally, in 1864 Aston Hall was sold to Birmingham Corporation and opened to the public and today it is run by Birmingham Museums and Art Gallery.

St Philip's Cathedral

The Church of St Philip was designed by Thomas Archer, known as the 'gentleman architect'. Work

St Philip's Anglican Cathedral was designed in the Baroque style by Thomas Archer. The church was consecrated in 1715 and became Birmingham Cathedral in 1905. This photo was taken shortly after major restoration was completed in 1993 (overleaf).

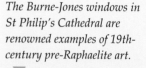

The Burne-Jones windows in St Philip's Cathedral are renowned examples of 19th-century pre-Raphaelite art.

commenced in 1709 and the main building completed in 1715. Archer had visited Rome for inspiration and this is reflected in the fine Roman Baroque detail of St Philip's, most particularly seen in the concave-sided tower. The tower and dome were completed later than the church, in 1725. Birmingham was granted city status in 1889 and St Philip's became a Cathedral in 1905.

A noteworthy feature of the interior is the excellent Pre-Raphaelite windows by Sir Edward Coley Burne-Jones. In the 1980s the Cathedral underwent major restoration which was finished in 1993. The weather-vane on the top of the dome incorporates a boar's head of the Gough-Calthorpe family crest. During restoration this was carefully dismantled and regilded with gold leaf.

Above all else St Philip's Cathedral is very welcoming and an ideal place to stop for a period of quiet reflection, right in the heart of the bustling city.

St Philip's Churchyard became a mass of flowers in September 1997 as people marked their feelings on the death of Princess Diana.

Soho House, Handsworth. *Now run as a museum, this was the home of Matthew Boulton from 1766 until his death in 1809. The house overlooked the famous Soho Manufactory which was just a short distance down the hill. Soho House was often a meeting place for the Lunar Society.*

Chapter Three
Boulton, Watt and Soho

T he industrial partnership of Matthew Boulton and James Watt played a significant role in Birmingham's development in the eighteenth century. The inventiveness of these industrialists, and their ability to turn ideas into manufactured products, enabled Birmingham to become a world leader in the supply of steam engines. The enterprise of Boulton and Watt was very important to the growth of Birmingham into a world centre for manufacturing in the eighteenth and nineteenth centuries.

Matthew Boulton, the son of a silver stamper and piercer, was born in Snow Hill, Birmingham in 1728. He became a partner in his father's business making Birmingham 'toys', the name given to items such as buckles, buttons and numerous other trinkets. From the outset Matthew wanted to remove the stigma attached to 'Brummagem' ware, by increasing the quality and reputation of Birmingham's products.

Investing on a Large Scale

In 1759 Boulton senior died and Matthew inherited the family business. He had already married Mary Robinson of Lichfield, who had an inheritance of £14,000. Sadly, she died at around the

◄

The statue of Boulton, Watt and Murdock, Broad Street, Birmingham.
(William Bloye, 1956).

same time as Matthew's father. The following year, at the age of thirty-two, he married Mary's sister Anne Robinson who came with an inheritance of a further £14,000. With this considerable financial security Boulton set about investing in manufacturing activities on a large scale and concentrating on good-quality products.

Boulton established the Soho Manufactory on Handsworth Heath, two miles to the north of Birmingham. The site already had a mill for metal processing and Hockley Brook had been diverted to form a millpond. Soho Pool, as the millpond became known, remained for a hundred years, until drained and filled in to make way for a

▲
Sarehole Mill.
Water mills were an important source of power for Birmingham industry. Matthew Boulton had an interest in Sarehole Mill before he built his famous Soho Manufactory at Handsworth. The Mill is open to the public during the summer months.

Sarehole Mill in action grinding corn, though originally it was probably for metal processing.

railway goods yard. The Soho Manufactory opened in 1764 and Boulton employed good-quality workmen. He was prepared to pay top wages to secure the right skills, a policy which attracted workers from all over Europe. High quality in design was equally encouraged. Boulton travelled to view work at the British Museum and also brought back examples of work from his foreign travels and his enthusiasm for good design quickly paid off. He even received loans of works of art from members of the aristocracy, who gave him much encouragement and support in his work. The Soho Manufactory produced Sheffield plate, silver plate and ormolu of the highest quality as well as the more mundane steel 'toys' such as buckles and buttons. The origins of both the Assay Office and the minting of coins in Birmingham emanated from the enterprise of Boulton (see chapter five).

Soho House

In 1761 Boulton purchased a small Georgian house on a hill-top overlooking the Soho Manufactory and this was his home from 1766 until his death in

1809. He greatly extended and redesigned the house and installed such innovations as central heating, a flush toilet and a hot water supply to the bath, all novelties for their day. Soho House, extensively renovated in 1993/4 is now a heritage centre run by Birmingham Museums and Art Gallery.

Power for the World

By 1770 the Soho Manufactory employed 800 workers, but only had two water wheels to power the equipment. Further expansion was severely limited by lack of power, with horses driving the mills at considerable expense whenever Hockley Brook dried up. Boulton had heard of attempts to use steam engine power and tried experiments himself, but nothing came of them. At the same time James Watt was working on new steam engine designs in Scotland. Watt started to call at Soho on the way home to Scotland from visits to London and was impressed with the quality of the work he saw. In 1770 Watt sent his first completed engine to the Soho Manufactory for testing and in 1774 came to work at Soho himself. With the

Birmingham 'toy making' is an ancient craft that continues in the city to this day. Here a promotional badge is seen in two stages of production at the firm of F.C. Parry, Highgate.

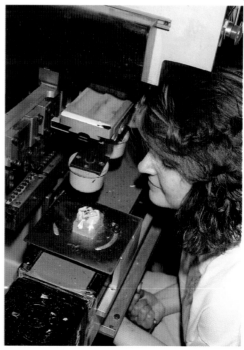

OPENING CEREMONY AT SOHO FOUNDRY BY MATTHEW BOULTON · 30 JANUARY · 1796

skilled Soho workforce, the inventiveness of Watt and the energy of Boulton, the steam engine design was perfected and Watt's earlier patent of 1769 was extended until 1800.

For twenty-five years Boulton and Watt produced most of the world's steam engines - approximately 500 engines in all. In 1778 they negotiated terms for steam-engine installations in Cornish tin mines, based on the amount of money saved compared with the conventional engines. Indeed, it was advances for powering the Cornish mines which alleviated a serious financial situation for the firm. Boulton, with his entrepreneurial flair, seemed largely untroubled by money problems, but Watt did not enjoy the continual financial insecurity.

The Invention of Gas Lighting

William Murdock called at the Soho Manufactory to ask for work. When Boulton heard that Murdock had turned his wooden hat on a home-made lathe, he was impressed and he was engaged the following day. Murdock was a very reliable engineer and spent many years in Cornwall taking charge of steam-engine installation. However, Murdock's greatest achievement was the invention of gas lighting. Following experiments using different types of coal to make gas, Murdock had his own house in Redruth lit by gaslight. He told Watt

The opening of the Soho Foundry.
The celebrations are portrayed in a mural to be found in the old Post Room of the Soho Foundry which is now part of Avery Berkel.

▶

Detail from the Smethwick Engine.
This 1778 Boulton and Watt engine was built to pump water back up the locks at Smethwick. It is still in working condition and will be displayed at Millennium Point, Digbeth.

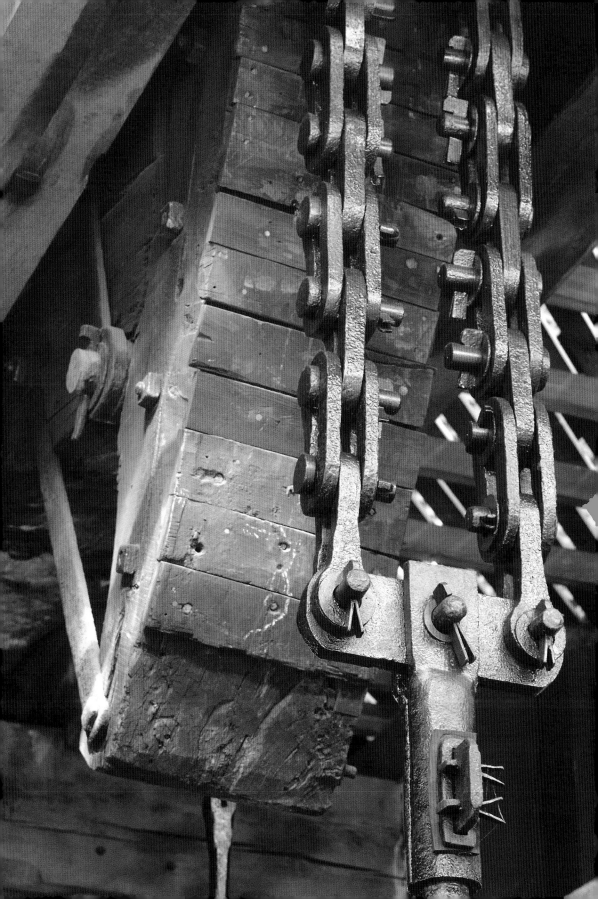

William Murdock's Cottage.
This is believed to have been his residence when he was based at the Soho Foundry.

of his invention and suggested a patent be taken out. However, the firm did not want to take on a new enterprise at that time and Murdock's discovery was not protected. The Soho Manufactory offices were lit by Murdock's invention and the manufacture of gas-making equipment was added to the list of products. The site of an early gasometer is still to be seen within the Soho Foundry, as is the cottage thought to have been used by Murdock. While living in Redruth Murdock also became interested in developing a steam carriage and in 1791 he produced a working model.

Boulton, Watt and Sons

James Watt Jnr. and Matthew Robinson Boulton, sons of the original partners, entered the business in 1794, the firm becoming Boulton, Watt & Sons. Though the steam-engine patent was coming to an end, there was a continuing demand for steam engines and in 1795 they bought land for development next to the canal in Smethwick, where the Soho Foundry was built. The opening of the Soho Foundry in 1796 was marked by a great feast which was attended by the engine-smiths and workers employed in constructing the new works.

Only two steam engines are known to survive from those built during the first phase of production of the Watt steam engine. One is 'Old Bess' an experimental engine used at the Soho Manufactory which was built in about 1777, and whose major components are now displayed in the Science Museum in London. The other is the Smethwick Engine of about 1778 which worked until 1892 pumping water back up the locks at Smethwick on the Birmingham Main Line canal. The Smethwick Engine was until recently a working exhibit at the Museum of Science and Industry and it will hopefully become a central exhibit at Millennium Point in Digbeth. Just along the canal from the original site of the Smethwick Engine, steam engines are still being manufactured on a large scale. Here, the Birmingham firm Mamod produces a sought-after collection of working model steam engines. Over fifty percent of their production is exported, with the Americas and Germany being strong markets.

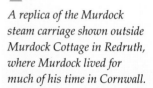

A replica of the Murdock steam carriage shown outside Murdock Cottage in Redruth, where Murdock lived for much of his time in Cornwall.

Mamod Steam Engine Production. Jackie Taylor solders a boiler while Peter Johnston assembles a steam powered bus.

After expiry of the steam-engine patent in 1800, the partnership of Boulton and Watt senior was dissolved and the two former partners continued quite separate lives. Watt retired to his home, Heathfield, in Handsworth and continued inventing. He devoted much of his time to constructing an art-carving machine, which could produce replicas of medallions and busts in either enlarged or reduced format. These were his so-called 'parallel eidographs'. He once wrote: 'If I live I hope to be able to produce a reduced copy of Chantrey's bust of myself, fit for a chimney piece as I do not think myself of importance enough to fill up so much of my friends' houses as the original bust does.'

In contrast to James Watt, Matthew Boulton continued to take an active interest in the firm after 1800. He died at the age of eighty-one in August 1809. At his funeral mourners included over 500 workmen from Soho, who were all presented with a commemorative medal. James Watt survived his friend and partner, dying in August 1819 at the age of eighty-three. Boulton and Watt are both buried in Handsworth Parish

Wattilisk
(Vincent Woropay, 1988);
Outside the Queen Elizabeth II Law Courts this sculpture is based on the art-carving machine invention developed by Watt during his retirement.

▶

St Mary's Church, Handsworth.
On the edge of Handsworth Park this was the family church attended by Matthew Boulton, James Watt and William Murdock, who are all buried there.

▼

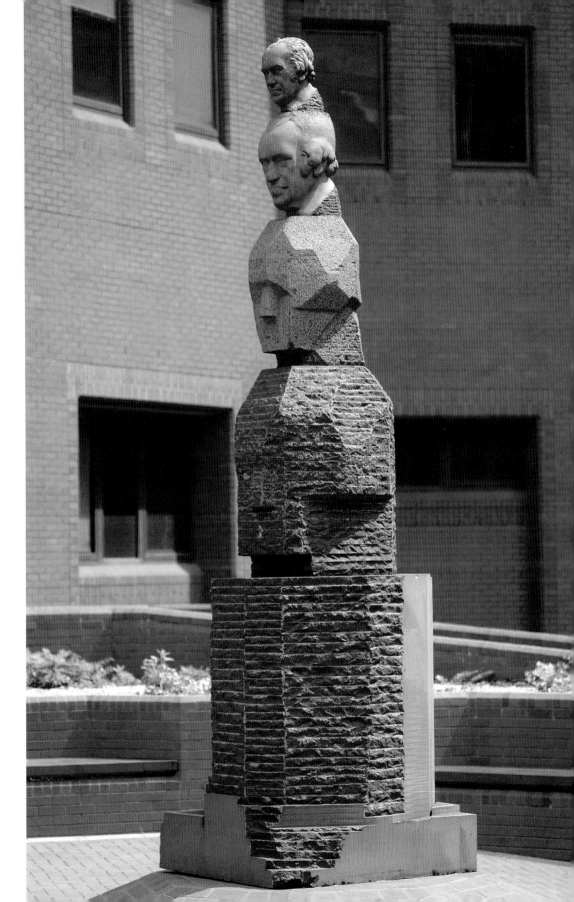

Church. On the walls of the church are busts of Boulton and Murdock but the chief piece is the sculpture of Watt by Francis Chantrey which was taken as a model for a more recent statue in Chamberlain Square.

Wattilisk, by Vincent Woropay, placed outside the Queen Elizabeth II Crown Courts just off Corporation Street, is based on the art-carving machine invention. Carved from black Indian granite, *Wattilisk* consists of five portrait heads, which are also based on the Chantrey bust of James Watt in Handsworth Parish Church. Only the uppermost head has the full features of Chantrey's original sculpture. As one moves down, each block becomes less finished, with the lowest one representing an early stage where the sculptor has just begun to determine the shape of the head.

The Lunar Society

Just try to imagine the scale and pace of change in eighteenth-century Birmingham. The coming of the canals, the new manufacturing processes and steam power were just a few of the new developments that those involved in commerce and industry had to keep pace with. A group of prominent progressive figures in and around Birmingham came together and became known as the Lunar Society. Its members, with different areas of expertise, were a highly influential philosophical group. They kept no minutes or records of their meetings but much has been learnt about their discussions from the letters of different members.

Meetings of the Lunar Society were held each month at full moon - hence its name - and its two founders were Matthew Boulton and Erasmus Darwin. Also members were James Watt and James Keir, an associate of Boulton who was involved in the chemical industry. Dr William Withering was best known for his discovery of the use of digitalis which was extracted from the foxglove and used in the treatment of heart disease. It is still in use today as the drug digoxin. (At one time Withering was said to be the highest-

The Lunar Society Room in Soho House includes the original table used for group meetings and a number of products of the Soho Manufactory.

paid physician outside London.) Other members of the group included Josiah Wedgwood and Joseph Priestley. The total membership of the Lunar Society was around fourteen people, though others were closely associated with the group.

The importance and success of the Lunar Society, due in part to the different professional backgrounds of the membership, is well illustrated by the election of eleven of its members as Fellows of the Royal Society. During its existence from 1766 to 1809 its influence extended far beyond local interests, indeed, well beyond England, and Benjamin Franklin, who became American President, was a close friend of some Lunar Society members. Today a modern-day Lunar Society exists and holds regular meetings to discuss relevant philosophical and historical matters.

Joseph Priestley is now remembered by a statue in Chamberlain Square, where he is depicted in his scientific role as the discoverer of oxygen (1774). However, besides being an eminent scientist of his time and member of the Lunar Society, Priestley was also a nonconformist minister and a radical. He became the minister of the New Meeting House in 1780, the Presbyterian place of worship which was well known for its liberal thinking. Priestley left Birmingham after riots which started on 14 July 1791 and which are now known as the Priestley Riots. To celebrate the second anniversary of the French Revolution, a dinner took place at a hotel in the centre of Birmingham. A mob gathered outside the hotel and violence erupted, with Priestley one of the main targets, even though he did not attend the dinner. The New Meeting House was burnt down and the mob then departed for Priestley's home in Sparkbrook which was destroyed along with his many items of laboratory equipment. Priestley finally left for New York in April 1794, where he spent the rest of his life lecturing and resuming his studies in chemistry.

The International Convention Centre canalside.

Chapter Four
Canals Rediscovered

Today Birmingham's canals are integral to city-centre redevelopment. Whether it is new houses, offices, convention centre or pub, a canal frontage is part of the Birmingham architect's brief. Where canals no longer exist they even discuss building them, mock locks and all and the proposed Arena Central development around the old Central TV studios will incorporate canals as an essential feature.

From the end of the Second World War until the 1970s the Birmingham canals were largely forgotten historical backwaters. Access was difficult, they were run down and only real enthusiasts made time to walk along these overgrown and hidden places. Now things are very different. In the late 1970s Birmingham City Council, the Department of the Environment and British Waterways within the Birmingham Inner City Partnership started to implement the city's Canal Improvement Programme. In the early 1980s towpaths were re-paved and access to canals was encouraged by the provision of doorways and new bridges. With the canals increasingly opened up for public use, a fascinating two-hundred-year-old story is now accessible for everyone to discover and enjoy.

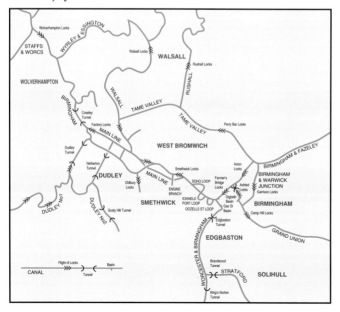

▶

The Guillotine Lock,
King's Norton.
At the Junction of the
Stratford Canal and the
Worcester and Birmingham
Canal this lock maintained a
6-inch difference in water
level right up to canal
nationalisation in 1948.

No Engineering Masterpiece

The original Birmingham canal system was built between the late 1760s and 1830. Canal transport of raw materials from the Black Country, notably coal and iron, was enormously important for Birmingham's industrial expansion. Work on the first canal between the Wednesbury coalfield and Birmingham town centre began in February 1768. The canal was surveyed by the great canal builder James Brindley, whose name now graces a pub in Gas Street Basin. This first section of canal was opened in November 1769. The arrival of Wednesbury coal in Birmingham had a dramatic effect, reducing coal prices by about 50 per cent in the town.

The canal between Birmingham and Wolverhampton was built by the Birmingham Canal Navigations Company (BCN) and was completed in September 1772. The original canal was not a civil engineering masterpiece, essentially following the contours of the land and winding in great loops to avoid expensive earth working. Though bringing great prosperity to Birmingham the canal

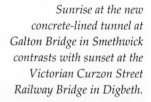

The Bond on the Warwick and Birmingham Canal in Digbeth. Originally the depot of canal carrying company Fellows, Morton & Clayton, this is now offices and the ground floor an exhibition venue.

Sunrise at the new concrete-lined tunnel at Galton Bridge in Smethwick contrasts with sunset at the Victorian Curzon Street Railway Bridge in Digbeth.

Gas Street Basin.

This is the meeting point of the Birmingham Canal Navigations and the Worcester and Birmingham Canal. The Worcester Bar is still present and now forms a pedestrian walkway which is closed at night to try to give remaining narrowboat dwellers some peace (previous page).

◀

was soon under pressure from the very large number of people trying to use it. Critics suggested that the excessive length of the canal had more to do with the fact that transport charges were based on 'cost per ton carried per mile' than anything else. The BCN Company was determined to control as much canal trade as possible. The shareholders were Birmingham industrialists and appeared to have two primary aims: to maximise profits on their canal and to ensure that the price of coal for use in their Birmingham factories was kept as low as possible. The BCN was a highly profitable concern declaring annual dividends as high as 70 per cent and by 1845 the original £140 shares were worth over £3,000.

Bars to Travel

The BCN soon extended its canal system with the Birmingham and Fazeley Canal going east and allowing connections with canal routes to London. Naturally enough, when an alternative route

▶

The James Brindley is a popular pub at Gas Street Basin.

▲

Warwick Bar.
This historic feature in the
Digbeth redevelopment
area has remained
unchanged for many years.

south, the Worcester and Birmingham Canal, was proposed in 1789, the BCN fought it hard. However, a Parliamentary act for this navigation was finally passed in 1791. In Birmingham the Worcester and Birmingham Canal terminated alongside the BCN canal to form Gas Street Basin, but the BCN Company insisted on a seven-foot-wide area of solid ground between the two canals. It was claimed that this was to prevent the Worcester canal from using up Birmingham's water. In reality the bar was a means of making it uneconomic to use the Worcester and Birmingham Canal to travel south, with the excessive transfer tolls and cranage levied by BCN. The Worcester and Birmingham Canal opened in October 1795 but, not surprisingly, the Company was beset by financial problems and the route to Worcester was not completed until 1815. The Worcester Bar in Gas Street Basin was a source of continual friction between the two canal companies. Eventually in July 1815 the stop lock was opened, but the BCN still continued to levy unreasonable tolls for many years. The stop lock and Worcester Bar can still be seen in Gas Street Basin, with the bar forming the path across the basin.

There are other examples of physical bars between canals owned by different companies. In Digbeth the Warwick Bar prevented unhindered crossing between the BCN Digbeth Branch to the Warwick and Birmingham Canal, which was later to become part of the Grand Union Canal. At King's Norton there is an unusual guillotine lock at the junction of the Stratford Canal and the Birmingham and Worcester Canal. This maintained a six-inch difference in water level between these two canals right up until canal nationalisation in 1948.

A narrowboat tour passes the National Indoor Arena at Old Turn Junction.

A Crooked Ditch

By the early 1820s the canal from Birmingham to the Black Country was suffering from acute congestion. Proposals for railways in Birmingham finally put pressure on the BCN Company to improve the canal through the Black Country to Wolverhampton. Thomas Telford was invited to survey the existing canal and was clearly unimpressed, commenting:

I found adjacent to this great and flourishing town a canal little better than a crooked ditch, with scarcely the appearance of a hauling path, the horses frequently sliding and staggering in the water, the hauling lines sweeping the gravel into the canal, and the entanglement at the meeting of boats incessant; while at the locks at each end of the short summit crowds of boatmen were always quarrelling or offering premiums for a preference of passage.

Telford's remedies included widening the Main Line, straightening the canal and building a new reservoir at Edgbaston to improve water provision. His plan included eight miles of new canal, completed in 1827, which reduced the journey between Birmingham and Wolverhampton by seven miles. However, despite the shorter distance, the BCN Company, in traditional style, continued to levy tolls based on the mileage of the old route.

Railway and Canal Side by Side

Eventually the railways led to the decline of canal transportation, but for many years canal and

Edgbaston Reservoir.
A good supply of water is critical to a successful canal system. In the 1820s Thomas Telford straightened the canal to Wolverhampton and this new reservoir was built at Edgbaston.
▼

railway flourished side by side. Between 1848 and 1898 the tonnage of goods carried on the canals nearly doubled, showing the benefit of both improving the canal system and integrating it with the newer railways.

In the twentieth century older industries which were based alongside the canal system, started to disappear. At the same time the increase in road and rail transportation of raw products and finished goods accelerated the decline in the Birmingham canal system. After the Second World War the future of the canals looked grim. Movement of goods onto the growing motorway network of the 1960s finally meant the end of commercial traffic on the Birmingham canal system. The British Transport Commission and local authorities could see no use for the canals and only the cost of filling them in saved the present 145 miles of Birmingham and Black Country canals.

Spaghetti Junction is a suitable symbol of the movement of transportation from rail to road.
▼

Gradually canal enthusiasts have increased in number and in the 1970s and 1980s the leisure use of canals rose very fast around the country. Although the Birmingham canals were not then a natural holiday centre because of their rather barren surroundings, this has now changed. An increased interest in industrial heritage has helped,

▲

The Soho Loop, close to City Hospital, has a keen angling club that meets on Sunday mornings. Fish such as roach and gudgeon are common catches.

◄

Reflections of the Gun Barrel Proof House at the Digbeth Canal Basin and an unusual view of the Rotunda.

Thomas the Tank Engine Day at Birmingham Railway Museum is a great day out. It was the coming of the railways and later the roads, that led to the gradual decline of commercial traffic on the canals.

▶

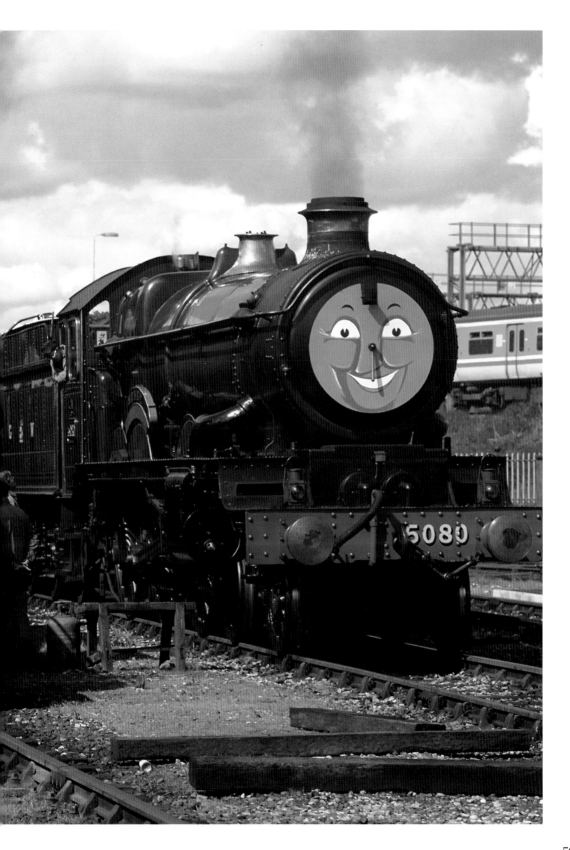

as has the major investment in the canal system and the surrounding environment, including towpath and lock reconstruction, dredging, provision of new moorings, and improved public access.

New Uses for Old Waterways

With their renewed economic and leisure use, canals have become central to many new developments in Birmingham. It is now possible to walk along newly renovated towpaths on all the Birmingham city-centre canals. Many people are taking advantage of the new environment in all sorts of ways. Landscaping has been undertaken and access improved on many parts of the canal; fishing is now possible with an increasing chance of success and these two-hundred-year canal corridors provide a haven for wildlife of all descriptions.

Interest in attracting people to live in the city centre has seen some major housing developments involving canal frontages. Symphony Court on the canal opposite the National Indoor Arena is a development of 143 new homes which includes some well-known names among the inhabitants. A very different example close-by has been the successful conversion of an old building at Sherborne Wharf into loft apartments.

Contrasting canalside developments: Hockley Port (below left) is a substantial and secure mooring for canal dwellers on the Soho Loop close to the city centre, while Sherborne Wharf (below) lies on a secluded loop of canal close to Brindleyplace.

Narrowboats are used as permanent homes in the city, the best known being those of the people who still manage to live in Gas Street Basin. Hockley Port is just a mile from the city centre on a quiet arm off the Soho Loop. Here British Waterways offers secure mooring facilities for narrowboat dwellers. Rent starts at about £1,000 a year for a full size mooring and around thirty people live on site. If you know where to look, you will find narrowboats moored on old arms of the canal system, no longer used by industry, in a number of places close to the city centre. About fifty people are thought to live on narrowboats in Birmingham itself with more in the surrounding areas.

City-centre canalside apartments and narrowboat living share the problem of safeguarding personal privacy while at the same time giving public access to canal towpaths. This has become much more of an issue with car parks and offices, sometimes overlooking prestige housing, offering rather too good a view into the luxury homes of football stars or those trying to cope with the after-effects of an arranged radio wedding.

In Bordesley Village, Heartlands, the canal again adds interest to a new housing development.

Twenty-First-Century Canals

Today the Birmingham canal system is at the heart of a new communications system and a fibre-optic cable has recently been installed beneath the entire towpath from London to Birmingham and beyond. This environment gives less chance of damage and disruption than running cable under congested roads. Further work has taken it north to Stafford and west along the Worcester and Birmingham Canal. This is a joint development by British Waterways and Fibreway. Over half this new national communications network will use canal corridors with the cable providing unlimited bandwidth for business and individual users.

The canal system in Birmingham and the Black Country helps to connect the National Cycle Network, a Millennium Commission project overseen by Sustrans, the Bristol-based civil engineering charity. In 1999 about ten people were cycling the Birmingham Canal Navigation towpath into Birmingham each day from the Black Country and perhaps half this number were coming along the Grand Union Canal from Solihull. As improvements are introduced canal towpath cycling for leisure and commuting increases dramatically.

Each spring sees city-centre workers running to work along the canal in preparation for the London Marathon. There is a long-distance path along the length of the Grand Union Canal from Gas Street Basin in Birmingham to Little Venice in London and many people have now walked or cycled its length.

Although carriage of goods on Birmingham canals has ceased, commercial traffic in the form of business seminars and tourist trips is now an everyday sight. Such trips get off to a good start with a safety announcement, which includes the encouraging statement; 'Don't worry, if the boat sinks just stand up and walk to the bank!'

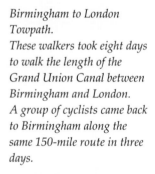

Birmingham to London Towpath.
These walkers took eight days to walk the length of the Grand Union Canal between Birmingham and London.
A group of cyclists came back to Birmingham along the same 150-mile route in three days.

New Year fireworks from Old Turn Junction.

Regeneration of city-centre canals and their integration into the city's leisure development in environmentally friendly ways has been recognised with several tourism awards. It is estimated that there are five million visits each year to the Birmingham canals and British Waterways now have a post of Tourism Development Officer for their Birmingham canals.

Interest in the history of the canals and their recreational use is growing all the time. There are considerable lengths of canal still to be re-developed, for example in Digbeth, with interesting Victorian buildings all around. Coming across the Warwick Bar or Digbeth Canal Basin, seeing the Gun Barrel Proof House from the canal or experiencing a Christmas Eve sunset reflected on the walls of Curzon Street railway bridge can make for an unforgettable walk. It is as you explore these more secret parts of the Birmingham canal system, that you appreciate the enormous potential the canals still offer for commercial and leisure development within the city.

The National Sealife Centre is part of the Brindleyplace development and attracts huge numbers of visitors to the city centre canalside. The building was designed by Sir Norman Foster and Partners and opened in June 1996.

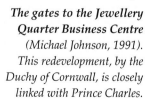

The gates to the Jewellery Quarter Business Centre *(Michael Johnson, 1991). This redevelopment, by the Duchy of Cornwall, is closely linked with Prince Charles.*

Chapter Five
An Urban Jewel

The Birmingham Jewellery Quarter is a ten-minute walk from the city centre and a fascinating area to visit and explore. It is a workplace, a rich source of industrial architecture, the site of a major Birmingham urban village scheme and an important centre for tourism. The jewellery industry has been established in Birmingham for around 200 years and almost from the start it has been concentrated in this one district.

In the nineteenth century, the Jewellery Quarter became a densely developed part of Birmingham. The industry relies on a marked division of labour with a multitude of specialist skills requiring the transfer of part-finished items between different craftsmen's workshops. The original development began when the Colmore family sold plots of land for building in the eighteenth century - Ann Colmore granted leases on parts of her estate from 1746 and Birmingham 'toy' makers moved into many of the houses with the area soon becoming a centre for this occupation. Later, in the mid-nineteenth century Colonel Vyse released land in a similar way. A large part of the Vyse Estate of villa-style residential housing was converted to commercial use and much of this can still be seen in the Quarter today. As the jewellery trade expanded, houses on these two estates were converted into multi-occupied business premises. These conversions often included the building of 'shopping' in the back yards and extensions at the front on upper levels - many of them still to be found in the Quarter.

The jewellery industry has always attracted small business enterprise, because so little capital investment was required for many of the crafts. An artisan needed a bench, or 'peg' as it was termed, and a few hand tools. Many different factors enabled the Birmingham Jewellery Quarter industries to develop and survive the periods of recession. The continued presence of the

▶

The Chamberlain Clock.
This commemorates the connection between the Jewellery Quarter and Joseph Chamberlain, who represented the area as an MP. Unveiled in 1904 by Mr and Mrs Chamberlain, the clock was purchased by public subscription to mark the efforts of Chamberlain in his services to the Empire in South Africa. The white building behind is the Big Peg.

▲

Mick Jones is a self-employed jeweller who specialises in ring mounting. Including a seven-year apprenticeship, he has worked in the Quarter for 40 years. He is seen here at one of the old Smith and Pepper benches in the Museum of the Jewellery Quarter soldering a ring.

Birmingham Assay Office, local engineering and tool-making expertise, the existence of precious-metal dealers and a ready gas supply, have all been important in the industry's survival.

The Assay Office

The Birmingham Assay Office first opened in 1773 in rented rooms above the King's Head public house in New Street and its existence was largely due to the petitioning of Parliament by Matthew Boulton. At that time his Soho Manufactory was starting to produce good-quality silverware but the goods had to be sent to the Chester Assay Office for hallmarking. This was both costly and inconvenient and meant that Birmingham products were not getting full recognition. The silver makers of both Birmingham and Sheffield petitioned Parliament together for their own Assay Offices. Despite opposition from London crafts-man, Boulton, who by then had considerable influence, managed to get the Act passed. Appropriately, it was items from the Soho Manufactory which were the first products to be handled by the new Assay Office.

Today the Birmingham Assay Office is in Newhall Street, opposite the former Museum of Science and Industry. The present building dates from 1877 and on one wall is the anchor mark, the Birmingham Assay Office Town Mark. It is thought that it was derived from the name of the Crown and Anchor Inn where much of the committee work was done in promoting the bill in Parliament. When Sheffield and Birmingham gained approval for their respective Assay Offices the story goes that the Town Marks were decided on the toss of a coin, Birmingham ending up with an anchor and Sheffield a crown.

Much of the growth of the Jewellery Quarter has been based on individual craftsmen who often worked as outworkers for larger traders. However,

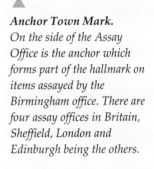

Anchor Town Mark.
On the side of the Assay Office is the anchor which forms part of the hallmark on items assayed by the Birmingham office. There are four assay offices in Britain, Sheffield, London and Edinburgh being the others.

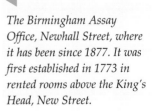

The Birmingham Assay Office, Newhall Street, where it has been since 1877. It was first established in 1773 in rented rooms above the King's Head, New Street.

The Birmingham Mint was started by Ralph Heaton and initially used equipment from the Soho Manufactory. The present building dates from 1861.

there have also been much bigger companies specialising in different areas of the jewellery trade. In particular, the process of electroplating was perfected in the Quarter and the firm of Elkington had a large factory on Newhall Street.

The Birmingham Mint

Another large-scale undertaking in the Jewellery Quarter has been the minting of coins and tokens. This activity was pioneered at the Soho Manufactory, by Matthew Boulton, where steam driven machines were used to produce coins for the reign of George III. The Soho coins were of a much better quality than those produced previously and did much to stop the output of forgeries, production of which had probably also been centred in Birmingham! Following this success, Boulton was contracted to install equipment at the Royal Mint, which was used for the next seventy years.

Painted Window, St Paul's Church
(Eginton, 1791).
Francis Eginton initially worked with Boulton at the Soho Manufactory. This fine painted window depicts the conversion of St Paul and is from the study of a painting by the American artist Benjamin West.

▼

The Birmingham Mint itself was established by Ralph Heaton who had expertise in the brass industry and 'toy' making, both important skills for minting coinage. He bought the Soho Manufactory minting equipment at auction and started to make coins for the home market and the colonies. The Mint moved to its present site in Icknield Street in 1860 and installed new machinery in the 1870s, which provided greater capacity than the Royal Mint in London. Indeed the Birmingham Mint was sub-contracted to do much of the Royal Mint's work, while they sorted out machinery problems in London. The size of the operation is illustrated by orders from Russia during 1896-98 which amounted to annual production of 110 million coins. Today the Birmingham Mint produces coins and blanks for many countries and medals and tokens for a wide range of markets. Having the foresight to re-equip with modern machinery at the right time has ensured the continued existence of the Mint. Indeed, it now has one of the world's foremost coin blank-plating facilities. Today the Birmingham Mint has the capacity for every part of coin production - initial casting of alloys is followed by milling, rolling and annealing after which blanks are cleaned and struck.

The Only Remaining Georgian Square

St Paul's Square in the Jewellery Quarter is the one remaining Georgian square in Birmingham. In the centre of the Square is St Paul's Church. Designed by the architect Roger Eykyn, it dates from 1779 and was built on land donated by Charles Colmore, who also gave £1,000 towards the cost of building. Further money for building the church was raised by selling freeholds for pew seats at £5 each. These were later re-sold and even bequeathed, and it took a hundred years for this seating to be released for general use. Matthew Boulton and James Watt both had pews, though their family church was St Mary's, Handsworth.

The fine painted east window was produced by Francis Eginton, who originally worked with Boulton at the Soho Manufactory before setting up his own workshops.

The houses of the square were originally built for residential use, but as the Jewellery Quarter expanded, this desirable district was slowly surrounded by factories, with many buildings in the square also being turned over to manufacturing. Recently the square became a conservation area and restoration of the old Georgian buildings and the church has been undertaken; many of the properties have been redeveloped yet again, this time for use as offices, restaurants or bars.

St Paul's Church was completed in 1779 and has been extensively renovated in the last few years. The church is often used for staging musical events, just as it was in the 18th century.

▶

Architectural Jewels

There is a wealth of interesting Victorian architecture to see in the Jewellery Quarter. The Argent Centre, on Frederick Street, one of the most attractive buildings in the Quarter, was constructed in 1863 for W. E. Wiley, a manufacturer of gold pens and pencils, and is built in the Renaissance style. The architect used hollow bricks and wrought iron ties in the construction, claiming that these

The Argent Centre was originally the Pen works of W.E. Wiley and is an excellent example of Jewellery Quarter architecture. It is now sub-divided into small business premises.

▼

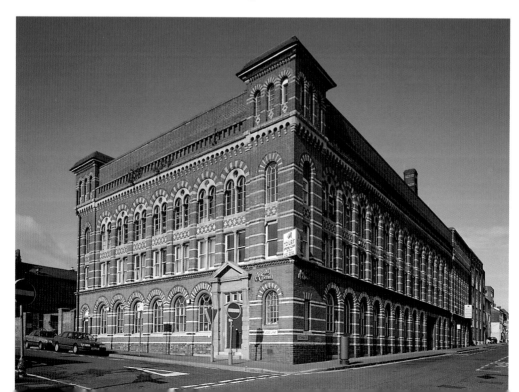

Pen Nib Works.
There is still evidence of a
surviving Birmingham pen
industry, which used to
dominate the world in the
19th century.

doubled the weight-bearing capacity of the floors and reduced the fire risk. The factory employed 250 workers in pen production and a further thirty-five used the excess steam from the factory to operate a Turkish bath. The building is now one of a number of centres providing small units for industrial and commercial use.

One of the best examples of the many redevelopments of Victorian buildings for modern use is the Jewellery Quarter Business Centre in Spencer Street which was undertaken by the Duchy of Cornwall and has been a focus for HRH the Prince of Wales's ideas on the regeneration of inner city areas. The development provides modern office and industrial premises for a wide range of different businesses. The £2.5 million development includes an unusual sculpture in the form of the entrance gates to the reception area. These are constructed from stainless steel and brass, a reference to the traditional silver and gold of the jewellery industry; cut glass 'jewels' are incorporated in the design which is meant to represent the 'tree of life'.

The former Hockley Centre is a large development, which was the result of 1960s ideas to try to redevelop the Jewellery Quarter. At that time many premises were in a very poor state of repair.

The School of Jewellery
frontage with Victorian, Arts
and Crafts and 1990s design.

It was thought that replacing them with a large modern building, sub-divided into units would encourage the interrelationships of craftsmen. The Hockley Centre, now renamed the 'Big Peg', has itself undergone renovation and has established a clearer identity within the Quarter.

Emphasis on Education

The Jewellery Quarter is still a major centre for production of jewellery, medals, badges and associated crafts. A School of Jewellery opened in 1890 and is still located in the Quarter, now as part of the University of Central England.

The building was recently redeveloped and was officially opened in 1995 with facilities for 600 students. The oldest part of the building was originally an 1860s workshop to which a third floor was added in 1906 and an arts-and-crafts style extension in 1911. Today's redevelopment by Associated Architects features an impressive longitudinal atrium linking the Victorian, Edwardian and modern components. The atrium brings light deep down into the building and the use of glazed partitions blurs distinctions between the different crafts.

An emphasis on education must be one of the reasons for the survival of the industry in the

Silver brooches by Lyn Antley with the special millennium hallmark added using a laser etching technique by Birmingham Assay Office.

Quarter. Employment in the Birmingham jewellery industry has always been relatively modest with a peak of perhaps 40,000 in 1913 which represented about 7 per cent of total employment in the city. In 1984 the industry was estimated to be employing about 5,000 workers.

A Tourist Centre

Once an area known only to those who had business there, the Quarter has more recently become a busy tourist centre. This has led to a large number of retail outlets opening and selling jewellery at bargain prices but today the number of individual craftsmen in the Jewellery Quarter also appears to be increasing. Their work is not always easy to find, though it is well worth taking the time to seek out the craftsmen among the larger discount jewellery outlets.

The Museum of the Jewellery Quarter is to be found at the premises of the former firm of Smith and Pepper, a traditional Jewellery Quarter business which closed in 1981. The premises were bought and preserved as they had been left, by Birmingham Museums and Art Gallery. This old works is now an award-winning museum which tells the fascinating story of the Quarter. Present-day Jewellery Quarter workers can be seen demonstrating their skills at the centre, which also retails an interesting range of work from local craftsmen.

Redevelopment Around the Corner

In 1998 it was estimated that some 26% of Jewellery Quarter land use consisted of vacant, derelict and cleared sites, with many significant buildings under-utilised. A short walk around today's Quarter shows that investment and sensitive redevelopment is required.

The development of an urban village in the Jewellery Quarter is now underway. The urban village concept has foundations of economic, environmental and social sustainability and the Prince of Wales has taken a lead in encouraging such ideas. The Urban Villages Forum, a key partner in the Jewellery Quarter Scheme, was established as part of his initiative. This significant development in the city centre follows urban village schemes at Bordesley and Bloomsbury as part of the regeneration of the Heartlands area.

The Jewellery Quarter Urban Village Board is charged with implementing the urban framework plan prepared for Birmingham City Council and the Urban Villages Forum. The Jewellery Quarter has considerable advantages for development as an urban village with its historic and distinctive character of streets evolved over several centuries. Interesting and varied architecture on a human scale lends itself to such development, and many buildings have already been adapted for different uses several times in their lifetimes. For the urban village designer this 'fine grain' environment is excellent material on which to build.

An Abandoned Jewellery Quarter factory in Vittoria Street close to the School of Jewellery. 'Views of the Big Peg and an excellent redevelopment opportunity'.

This derelict building in Legge Lane may be described as 'In need of modernisation overlooking the city centre'.

Designs for People

The Jewellery Quarter Urban Village will create a mixed-use urban development where people can live, work and find the necessities of daily life in an environment with a strong identity. Despite its wealth of adaptable architecture only about 700 people live in the Quarter; housing projects aim to increase the local population to about 5,000 with new housing catering for the full range of people interested in city-centre living. Local facilities, such as shopping, education and healthcare will be incorporated into new development.

All that Glisters

In 1999 a public art project was organised in the Quarter. The project, given the name 'All that Glisters', involved six very different commissions. The most visual was a sixty-foot photographic work on the side of the Big Peg. Named SL-4 this comprised photographic images of the city centre taken from the top of the Big Peg, which were superimposed on a plastic mannequin's face and printed onto fabric.

In an empty shop frontage Pat Kaufman used a mixture of Jewellery Quarter furniture, light and reflections to produce a room that 'time forgot'.

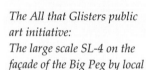

The All that Glisters public art initiative:
The large scale SL-4 on the façade of the Big Peg by local artist Lee Lapthorne.

Chicago-born Pat Kaufman's shop front at Turley's workshop in Warstone Lane.

The idea was re-enforced by layers of dust and the jumbled objects made even more mysterious by the reflection of Warstone Lane in the shop window. Other unusual installations used buildings around the Quarter and this event drew attention to the area at the start of the urban village project.

Birmingham Gun Quarter

Gun-making also involves the interaction of a number of specialised craftsmen. In Birmingham the production of hand-made guns became centred on an area close to St Chad's Cathedral. By the end of the seventeenth century Birmingham was supplying 200 muskets a month to the Government and during the Napoleonic Wars three million gun barrels were made in the town. Birmingham supplied almost every firearm in the country until the 1880s when Belgian imports began to encroach and the ordinance factory at Enfield was established. Guns were tested at the Proof House, which was built in 1813, and is still to be found in Banbury Street backing on to Digbeth Canal Basin.

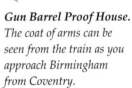

Gun Barrel Proof House.
The coat of arms can be seen from the train as you approach Birmingham from Coventry.

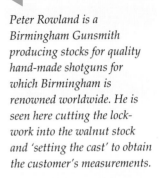

Peter Rowland is a Birmingham Gunsmith producing stocks for quality hand-made shotguns for which Birmingham is renowned worldwide. He is seen here cutting the lock-work into the walnut stock and 'setting the cast' to obtain the customer's measurements.

In 1861 the Birmingham Small Arms (BSA) factory opened in Small Heath and large-scale Birmingham gun-making moved away from small workshop production. The craft of hand-made specialist gun-making has continued, though the inner ring road, built in the 1960s, swept through and destroyed the heart of the Gun Quarter. However, there are visible signs that the industry continues and sporting guns made in Birmingham still have an excellent reputation.

The Ikon Gallery, Oozells Square at Brindleyplace, was originally Oozells Street Board School (Martin and Chamberlain, 1877). Restoration was undertaken by Levitt Bernstein Associates (1998).

Chapter Six

Victorian and Modern

Successful cities respond to change and in doing so must adapt their buildings to suit modern-day requirements. Historically in Birmingham the way forward has been to level the place every so often as the needs of the city change. This process continues but today there is a greater appreciation that inherently good design from previous generations should where possible be retained and adapted for modern use. Birmingham's architecture is clearly rooted in the Victorian era and here we look at this aspect as well as some major projects in today's city.

In the late nineteenth century terracotta was used for linings both outside and inside buildings. These decoratively moulded clay blocks offered bright colours, usually red or buff, good resistance to corrosion from smoke and soot, and sharpness of intricate detail that could not be achieved using carved stonework. Terracotta production was centred on Midland towns around Birmingham. However, many of the most distinctive red façades were manufactured at Ruabon, North Wales, known as 'terracottopolis', where the plentiful clay supplies were a by-product of mining.

Moulded terracotta linings began to be used in façades with carved stone. A good example of this is Oozells Street School on Broad Street, which was built in 1878 and now forms part of the Brindleyplace development. Tiled pavements, a forerunner of terracotta, can be seen in the 1840 work by Minton in St Chad's Cathedral.

Architecture to Express Ideals

If terracotta was the physical way of expressing new ideals then Joseph Chamberlain was the man who helped make it all happen. Like a number of other influential Birmingham citizens, Chamberlain was not Birmingham born, but a Londoner who came to Birmingham in 1854 to help in the screw-making factory of his uncle, J.S. Nettlefold. The firm wanted to introduce new American equipment to

St Chad's Cathedral was designed by the leading architect of the Gothic revival, A.W. N. Pugin (1840). It pre-dates the use of terracotta.

▶

Early tiled pavements by Minton dating from the 1840s can be seen in St Chad's Roman Catholic Cathedral. They are an example of the collaboration between Minton and A.W.N. Pugin.

▼

Statue to George Dawson
(T. Woolner, 1885).
*George Dawson (1821-1876)
was one of a group of free-
church radical ministers who
preached the Civic Gospel
and Joseph Chamberlain was
among his congregation.*

▶ ▶

*Detail from the façade of
Spring Hill Library shows the
city coat of arms. Comparison
with today's version in
Victoria Square shows some
interesting differences.*

improve production and he required additional capital for his venture. He approached Chamberlain senior for financial help and his son, Joseph Chamberlain, arrived in Birmingham as part of the deal.

The town that Chamberlain came to work in was clearly suffering as a result of enormous industrial expansion. By the mid-nineteenth century Birmingham had become the major hardware manufacturing centre of the world. The largely uncontrolled industrial growth and urban expansion had brought great social and economic problems. People worked long hours in unhealthy and dangerous conditions, returning home to poor-quality housing, which lacked basic amenities such as a clean water supply and sewage disposal and the town still had 50,000 back-to-back houses. It is not surprising that in inner-city districts, 20 per cent of children died before they were old enough to walk.

The Nettlefold firm began to make large profits based on new manufacturing processes and the company came to dominate the wood screw market. This success enabled Chamberlain to spend time considering the problems of the living and working conditions around him in Birmingham. He was influenced by the Lancashire radical John Bright, who became a Member of Parliament for Birmingham in 1857. The teachings of preachers such as George Dawson were also highly influential in the development of ideas that became known as the 'Civic Gospel' and which led to a period of unparalleled change in the town.

Radical Change Soundly Financed

Chamberlain was particularly interested in improvements to education. In 1869, he became a Town Councillor for St Paul's ward in the Jewellery Quarter, becoming a member of the Birmingham School Board in 1870 and Mayor of Birmingham in 1873. In a speech as Mayor, he set

▲

Spring Hill Library.
This is an excellent example of graceful Gothic design and includes intricate terracotta detail (Martin and Chamberlain, 1893).

out his aims for a radical programme of improvements and he promised that the town 'shall not, with God's help, know itself!'.

Purchase of the two gas companies and the waterworks by the Council helped finance municipal development. The grandest scheme of Chamberlain's Council, known as the Improvement Scheme, involved the demolition of ninety acres of slums in the town centre together with the development of Corporation Street. Chamberlain was as astute in municipal finances as he had been in manufacturing. Payments on the leases on the newly constructed Corporation Street shops and offices soon recovered the costs for that scheme.

When after three years as Mayor, Chamberlain was elected a Member of Parliament he took a London residence near Hyde Park and also had a house built in Birmingham, named Highbury after his childhood home in London. John H. Chamberlain, (no relation to Joseph Chamberlain) was responsible for the design of Highbury. With his partner William Martin, John H. Chamberlain was at the forefront of new building design in Birmingham during the 'municipal revolution'.

Highbury, the home of Joseph Chamberlain, designed by John H. Chamberlain (no relation) and completed in 1880, uses a mixture of stone and plaster as well as terracotta. John H. Chamberlain was a follower of Ruskin and his designs were richly decorated. Highbury is now owned by Birmingham City Council and is opened to the public several times a year.

▼

Schools to Look Up to

With the Education Act of 1870 many schools and educational institutions were built and these new schools contrasted with the densely packed, poor-quality dwellings surrounding them. During this period the firm of Martin and Chamberlain were the architects responsible for forty-one board schools up to 1898, though John H. Chamberlain himself died in 1883 at the age of fifty-two. They favoured the Gothic style and used deep red brick and terracotta, with towers that often rose to a considerable height. This architectural partnership almost had a monopoly on the design of public buildings in Birmingham such as free libraries, public baths, asylums and water-pumping stations. Many of these buildings are still in excellent condition. Spring Hill Library has a large tower and the terracotta detail includes the city coat of arms. This is now beside a busy round-about, or 'island' as they are called in Birmingham. Free libraries first came to Birmingham in 1861 and by 1911 there were eleven in the city.

▲

Oozells Street School as it was in 1992. Comparison with the restored building on page 83 reveals the attention to detail in the 1990s renovation.

◀

Ladypool Junior and Infant School
(Martin and Chamberlain). This impressive building is just one of many such school buildings that can still be seen around the city. Note the ventilation shaft incorporated into the Gothic design.

Victoria Law Courts

Corporation Street was the most dramatic demonstration of the Civic Gospel. Although much has gone, the Aston end still has a striking group of terracotta decorated buildings. These include the Victoria Law Courts (1887-91), the General Hospital (1892-7), now the Children's Hospital, and the Methodist Central Hall (1899-1903). The Victoria Law Courts, are a fine example of the use of terracotta, the typical red on the outside contrasting with the yellow-brown in the great hall inside.

Terracotta to Drink in

Richly decorated terracotta helped to impress local building officials and licensing justices. The 1890s saw a major redevelopment and expansion of public houses in Birmingham. Between 1889 and 1914 terracotta was used on about twenty-six Birmingham pubs which were mainly the work of the architects James and Lister Lea and also William Jenkins, with the Hathern Station Brick and Terracotta Company. Much of the detail on the façades of these pubs reflects the prolific artistic expression of the Hathern staff.

An imposing red brick and terracotta building in Great Hampton Street. Built in 1896, it served as a memorial to Lord Roberts of Kandahar, Commander in Chief of the British Empire.

▶

The Red Lion Public House, Soho Road, Handsworth, was designed in 1902 by James and Lister Lea, who were responsible for many of the terracotta pubs in Birmingham.

◀

The Victoria Law Courts (Aston Webb and Ingress Bell, 1887-91), at the end of Corporation Street, display intricate use of terracotta in a mixture of architectural styles.

Developments on Broad Street

The last decades of the twentieth century have seen grand redevelopment projects in Birmingham, mainly concentrated on the west side of the city centre, including Centenary Square, the International Convention Centre and Brindleyplace, which have also helped to rejuvenate the areas around them. Indeed, the whole of the Broad Street area is experiencing an enormous renaissance. The latest proposals are to transform the six-acre site around the former Central Television studios and Alpha Tower into a glass-covered 24-hour leisure complex called Arena Central. Plans include a skyscraper and a proposed canal extension into Arena Central from Gas Street Basin to form a major water feature.

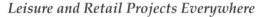

Number Three Brindleyplace (Porphyrios Associates, 1998). The atrium (above) gives a pleasing working environment. This is a welcoming building, made the more so by friendly front-desk staff.

Leisure and Retail Projects Everywhere

In 1999 Birmingham's largest building, the Royal Mail Sorting Office, was handed over to developers with the sorting office moving to a new facility in Heartlands. The Mailbox, as the development is known, is located on the Worcester and Birmingham

Brindleyplace Bar is a central feature in The Square at Brindleyplace (Piers Gough, 1997).

◄ The Left Bank restaurant on Broad Street is an interesting use of a former Barclays Bank. During the G8 Summit the leaders' wives dined here and the safe, still in position in the middle of the room, would have been a cause for comment.

Canal and plans include a new public square with shops, hotels, offices, roof-top apartments and canalside restaurants and bars.

Broadway Plaza retains the façade of the former Birmingham Children's Hospital to create a leisure, retail and residential complex at the end of Broad Street, including a central piazza, multi-screen cinema and up to 65 loft-style apartments. The Children's Hospital itself has been moved to the former General Hospital building in Steelhouse Lane close to the site of the first Children's Hospital, which opened in 1862.

The site of Birmingham Children's Hospital in Ladywood is levelled as work begins on Broadway Plaza.
An open day marked the opening of the newly converted Children's Hospital in Steelhouse Lane in 1998.
▼

Focus on St Chad's

City-centre living of different kinds is evident at St Chad's Circus close to Snow Hill Station. By the side of the Birmingham and Fazeley Canal, Focus Foyer, Birmingham's first foyer project, opened its doors in 1998. In a building of distinctive design it offers up to 80 young people a study bedroom and training resources. Situated on busy city-centre roads the bedrooms face inwards to overlook a quiet courtyard. Foyers are a French idea to tackle homelessness by providing accommodation together with training, careers guidance, personal development and job search facilities. This successful project uses these ideas in an innovative way and involves both public and private-sector organisations.

Close to the Focus Foyer is City Heights, a development of 82 one-and-two bedroom flats. This is a bold project to create quality private housing in what has until now been an unlikely site for private residential development. City Heights has proved popular in encouraging other housing developers to consider similar city-centre housing projects.

▶

St Chad's Circus.
(overleaf)
On the far left is the red brick City Heights, one of many examples of city-centre living developments with Focus Foyer in the centre next to St Chad's Cathedral.

The Kennedy Memorial in the centre of St Chad's Circus (Kenneth Budd, 1967).

▼

Bull Ring and More

As Birmingham enters the 21st century emphasis is gradually shifting to the east side of the city. By 1999 the redevelopment of the Bull Ring had been at the planning stage for a decade. The 1960s-built Bull Ring comprised markets, a shopping complex and offices all of which are to be levelled once more, with a new Bull Ring to be created on the site, though the Rotunda will be retained. In February 1999 developers Hammerson, Henderson Investors and Land Securities formed The Birmingham Alliance to jointly redevelop the Bull Ring and Martineau Square areas.

The new Bull Ring will have a major new public square around St Martin's Church, which will be restored as part of the project. The shopping development will include department stores and over a

The Rotunda was
designed by James
Roberts, and is an icon
to the 1960s wealth of
Birmingham. It is now
to be integrated into
redevelopment of the
Bull Ring area of
the city.

100

◄ ▲

The Bull Ring site from the top of the Rotunda and the model of the Bull Ring development shown to Birmingham citizens in 1999.

Work begins on the Millennium Point site in June 1999.

▼

hundred shops with an integral new bus station and links to New Street and Moor Street railway stations. Bull Ring developers have the difficult task of rebuilding a much-loved part of central Birmingham and also fulfilling retailers' aspirations. Overall the Birmingham Alliance would appear to be successfully addressing this complex situation. Work started in 1999 on the new indoor market hall, with the old Bull Ring to be demolished during 2001 and completion projected for 2003.

The Martineau Galleries scheme includes up to eighty shops and leisure facilities with the first phase commencing in 2000. Situated between the Bull Ring and Martineau Galleries schemes, the Masshouse district is an under-used area of open car parking beneath the raised inner ring-road. Plans for Masshouse make most of the natural contours of the sandstone ridge and will bring the ring-road back to ground level, converting it into a boulevard-style road. The area will form an important link between Millennium Point, the city centre and development opportunities in Digbeth.

Millennium Point

In 1999 the redevelopment of one part of Digbeth got underway with the start of the Millennium Point project, a multi-faceted technology-based scheme on a twelve-acre site close to the city centre and Aston University campus. Partners in the scheme are Birmingham City Council, the University of Central England (UCE) and Birmingham Chamber of Commerce and Industry. Funding includes £50 million from the Millennium Commission as well as the European Regional Development Fund, Advantage West Midlands, partners and sponsorship.

Curzon Street Station (Philip Hardwick, 1838). This was the terminus of the London to Birmingham railway and overlooks Millennium Point.

Millennium Point contains a number of independent but inter-linked elements. The Discovery Centre looks to the future and also celebrates the scientific and technological achievements of Birmingham and the West Midlands. It will use new-style interactive technology and virtual reality simulations. Well-known exhibits from the former Museum of Science and Industry in Newhall Street, including the working Smethwick Engine (Watt & Boulton, 1778) and the City of Birmingham steam locomotive, will be installed in the Discovery Centre. The overall aim is to make science and technology fun to experience and anyone who has visited the Light on Science Gallery at the Museum and Art Gallery will appreciate the potential for the hands-on approach to science.

The University of the First Age will provide educational opportunities for a regional audience with an electronic network linking schools, colleges, libraries, homes and the workplace. The primary focus will be to help with out-of-school learning for 11-to-15 years olds.

The Technology Innovation Centre is an initiative led by UCE that will house the Engineering and Computer Faculty. It aims to be a centre of excellence with an emphasis on access and participation by young people and industry. The Hub

will be a social centre providing shops, cafes, electronic library and a wide-screen format theatre. Millennium Point will be completed in 2001 and is expected to create many jobs and aims to attract over one million visitors a year.

Digbeth Millennium Quarter

Digbeth is the historic birthplace of Birmingham. The River Rea, now largely lost in a concrete culvert, runs through an area that has changed little for many years. The 1960s inner-ring road has helped to preserve a wealth of interesting architecture with considerable potential. As city-centre projects proceed the Digbeth area will become attractive to developers and a planning structure is intended to ensure that change is co-ordinated.

Digbeth is still predominantly an industrial area with traditional industries in Digbeth and Sparkbrook including large metal-finishing concerns such as electro-plating. There are also extensive unexploited spaces in Digbeth and proposals include new urban village schemes, close to Warwick Bar. For the urban developer the regeneration of Digbeth offers a huge opportunity

The River Rea is largely hidden from view and runs in a culvert through Digbeth. The inner ring road at Masshouse has been an effective barrier for the spread of city centre development.

The Custard Factory, Digbeth. Originally the home of Bird's Custard this is now the home to companies specialising in media and the arts.

for conversion of interesting architecture for modern-day use as well as sites for brand new buildings.

Bold Planning Rewarded

Birmingham continues to place greater emphasis on architectural integrity and sound urban design as projects proceed. The city does not want to repeat past mistakes and a worthwhile discussion between citizens, planners and developers is an important part of the planning process. City developments in the last two decades of the twentieth century have been successful and continue on a large scale and this period of enlightened change in Birmingham is still gaining momentum; if it continues at this pace it will compare in scale to changes in the late Victorian era.

▲

British Metal Treatments is based alongside the canal in Sparkbrook and specialises in electroplating chromium, copper and nickel deposits onto large items. Here are seen stages in the electroplating and finishing of a worn printing-press roller.

▶

Centenary Square at Night
The Forward Statue (Raymond Mason, 1991), looks to the entrance of the International Convention Centre where the canopy contains the neon sculpture Birdlife (Ron Haselden, 1991).

Chapter Seven
Art on the Streets

Public art is not a new concept in Birmingham and there are many examples to see in the city dating from Victorian times. Even older is the bronze statue of Lord Nelson by Richard Westmacott in the Bull Ring, one of the earliest monuments to Nelson in Britain (1809).

However, as Birmingham has undergone redevelopment, a great deal of attention has recently been given to public art. This now requires proper examination. The concept of setting aside a proportion of the capital costs of a building

Lord Nelson Statue
(Richard Westmacott,1809)
An old public statue in
the Bull Ring.

▼

programme to help fund public art projects has provided many works of art. Birmingham has been at the forefront of the 'per cent for art' initiative, applying it during the building of the International Convention Centre and Centenary Square. Following this success, public art has been integrated into the redevelopment of Victoria Square, Old Square and Brindleyplace. It has also been incorporated into other projects such as the Heartlands development, to the east of the city centre.

▲

One of four bronze sculptures by Albert Toft seen round the Hall of Memory in Centenary Square (1923-24).

Centenary Square

Centenary Square was designed by artists Tess Jaray and Tom Lomax in conjunction with City Council Architects and was completed in 1991. Paving designs and other features such as seating, lighting, railings and plants have all been integrated into the design for the Square.

Speaking of her Centenary Square work Tess Jaray said:

> *I discovered that the differences between conceiving a painting and conceiving an idea for an actual site are not as great as they might first appear. Therefore, the proposal for Centenary Square was always seen as a total concept, as a painting must be. Every aspect, each element, must function in its own right, for its own purpose, but still be part of the whole.*

Within this integrated concept of a square there are also a number of more formal works of art. Each is quite different, but one thing they have in common is the feel of a city that is both prepared to take stock of its past and is looking forward to the future in a very positive way.

Don't Forget the Past

There are several works of art in Centenary Square which have been around for many years. Round the Hall of Memory (1923-4) are four sculptures in bronze by Albert Toft. Across Broad Street, outside the Registry Office, is a sculpture by William Bloye

▶

New Year Fireworks in Centenary Square. The first New Year Party in Centenary Square marked the start of 1992 and the Sounds Like Birmingham year of music. An estimated 50,000 people enjoyed the spectacle.
(overleaf)

▲

Bloye's statue of Boulton, Watt and Murdock in front of the Registry Office with Alpha Tower in the background.

erected in 1956. This is a larger-than-life represen-tation of the famous eighteenth-century Birmingham industrialists Boulton, Watt and Murdock.

Forward into the Future

A more controversial piece of public art in Centenary Square, is the statue *Forward* by Raymond Mason (1991). Taking its name from the city's motto, *Forward* was cast in resin at the Haligon Studios near Paris. Mason was Birmingham born and worked with Bloye when he was Master of Modelling at Birmingham School of Art. He moved to France in the 1940s and has become internationally known for his large-scale figurative sculptures. For his home city he has represented the onward march of the people of Birmingham. Backed by the power-house of the city's industry the figures grow in size towards the front, where a worker holds up his industrial hand. Included among the figures are the Chamberlains and the Lady of the Arts from the city coat of arms, seen throwing a kiss to the past, while an actress offers a bouquet to the Birmingham Repertory Theatre across the Square.

The *Forward* statue has stimulated a widening public discussion on art in the City of Birmingham and on these grounds alone it must be considered a success, but it has met with a mixed response from the Birmingham public. Perhaps one should remember that when Bloye's statue of Boulton, Watt and Murdock was put up in Broad Street it was described as representing 'Mr Lee and Mr Longland selling a carpet or inspecting a roll of wallpaper', Lee Longlands being an old estab-lished department store close by in Broad Street.

Enterprise Cast in Bronze

There are three further contemporary works of art in Centenary Square. Centrally placed is the Tom Lomax water sculpture *The Spirit of Enterprise* (1991) which has three large sand-cast bronze dishes

Detail from the
Forward statue .

▶

Forward, Centenary Square
(Raymond Mason, 1991), is
constructed from fibreglass,
with resin and polymer paint,
and is centrally positioned in
Centenary Square.

▼

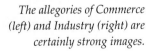

Spirit of Enterprise
(Tom Lomax, 1991)
Three great bronze dishes support allegories of Commerce, Industry and Enterprise.

The allegories of Commerce (left) and Industry (right) are certainly strong images.

supporting allegories of Commerce, Industry and Enterprise. Lomax intended the flow of water through the sculpture to indicate the passage of time, with the circles portraying symbols of eternity and the cascade of water down the curved steps helping to integrate the fountain with the surroundings.

Monument to John Baskerville

Outside Baskerville House is David Patten's Portland stone and bronze sculpture *Monument to John Baskerville - Industry and Genius* (1990), which lies close to the site of Easy Hill, the residence of John Baskerville. As an influential eighteenth-century Birmingham industrialist Baskerville had two quite different driving forces. He was an entrepreneur, making his fortune from

▶

Industry and Genius
(David Patten, 1990)
A representation of the Baskerville type-punches, spells out the title (in reverse) of the first work printed by Baskerville.

△

Symphony Hall Mural
(Deanna Petherbridge,1991).
Detail.

Construction: An Allegory
(Vincent Woropay, 1992).

▽

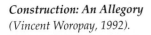

various manufacturing ventures including japanning and papier-mâché production, but he is best remembered for developing a stylish typeface and using it to print classical works on his printing press. The printing side of his business seems to have been only marginally profitable and perhaps he pursued it as much to satisfy an artistic urge. His first book, *The Poems of Virgil*, was produced in 1757 and sold at a guinea.

Although Baskerville was a non-believer he took great pains to publish the Common Prayer Book and the Bible. He became the printer to Cambridge University in December 1758 and completed a magnificent folio Bible in 1763.

Baskerville died on 8 January 1775 at the age of sixty-nine and at his request was buried in a vertical position in his garden. On his monumental urn it read: 'Stranger - beneath this cone, in unconsecrated ground a friend to the liberties of mankind directed his body be inurn'd.' Today the body lies in the catacombs of Warstone Lane cemetery.

Industry and Genius symbolises the type-punches for letters in the Baskerville typeface, spelling out the title of his first book, Virgil, in reverse.

Public Art in the International Convention Centre

Inside the ICC there are a number of pieces of public art. *Birdlife* (1991) is a neon sculpture incorporated into the canopy at the front entrance of the ICC. By Ron Haselden, this 'living' multi-coloured neon represents an abstract tree growing up through an aviary. The movement of the sculpture is computer-controlled and simulates the migration of birds, perhaps symbolising international travel.

On the canalside of the ICC is a large abstract stained glass design by Alexander Beleschenko (1991). It contains over 50,000 pieces of hand cut and shaped coloured glass and is encased between two sheets of toughened clear glass.

This abstract Stained Glass Window is found above the canalside entrance to the International Convention Centre (Alexander Beleschenko, 1991).

Other works of art on display in the ICC include *Construction: An Allegory* by Vincent Woropay (1992), *Symphony Hall Mural*, an oil mural on four floors by Deanna Petherbridge and *The Convention*, a wooden sculpture on the wall on the Symphony Hall side of the Mall by Richard Perry.

Chamberlain Square

There are several works of public art from Victorian times in Chamberlain Square. The Chamberlain Memorial Fountain was constructed from Portland stone and erected in 1880, shortly after Chamberlain left local Government to take up his seat in Parliament. There are also statues to James Watt and Joseph Priestley.

Birdlife
(Ron Haselden, 1991).

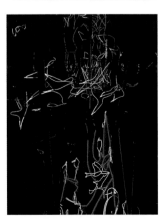

In 1993 a new sculpture of Thomas Attwood was sited in Chamberlain Square. The figure is cast in bronze and seen reclining on the steps of the square alongside a soap-box and sheets from one of the great politician's speeches. Born in Halesowen in 1783, Attwood was a Birmingham banker and MP. He founded the Birmingham Political Union which pressed for currency and parliamentary reform. He was a prime mover for the Reform Bill of 1832, which allowed Birmingham to elect two MPs, but he withdrew from public life after the Chartist Riots. By the time of his death he had fallen from favour and was largely forgotten. In more recent times his considerable influence on economic thinking and democratic reform has once again been recognised. An earlier statue of Thomas Attwood was moved from the city centre to Sparkbrook near the site of his house.

Old Square Resurfaces

Birmingham has a fascination with creating public squares. Recently Old Square has been converted from intimidating subways to a much more people-friendly ground-level environment. The

original Old Square dates from 1713 when it consisted of sixteen grand houses with a central space, but this was lost in the late Victorian era with the building of Chamberlain's Corporation Street. Today the square is overlooked by some interesting office developments, including the converted Lewis's department store building. Old Square is an important link between city-centre districts and contains some unusual public art.

The comedian Tony Hancock was born in Hall Green and was one of the great 1960s comedians until his untimely drink-and drug-related death in 1968. The Hancock tribute in Old Square comprises numerous glass rods running through a bronze base. The image itself is taken from the 1960 photo of Hancock by Joan Williams, with Hancock wearing his familiar coat and homburg hat and with a cup of tea.

Old Square with The Minories office development, originally the Lewis's department store, in the background.

▼

The Memorial to Tony Hancock (Bruce Williams, 1996) was unveiled by Sir Harry Secombe.

An interesting mural originally sited in the Old Square subway is much better for being renovated and brought to the surface. This mural, by Kenneth Budd, is one of a number he was commissioned to produce for inner-ring road developments in 1967-8, Other notable examples are the J.F. Kennedy Memorial (see page 95) and the History of Snow Hill murals at St Chad's Circus.

Old Square Mural (Kenneth Budd, 1967). Originally sited in the subway this mural considers the history of Old Square.

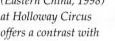

The Oriental Pagoda (Eastern China, 1998) at Holloway Circus offers a contrast with the BT Tower.

The youthful Hebe (Robert Thomas, 1966) at Holloway Circus.

Gateway to Chinatown

A different approach to the inner-ring road has been taken at Holloway Circus, where the subways have been maintained under this busy roadway but where the central space has been transformed. In 1998 a forty-foot high Chinese pagoda was installed. Made by craftsmen in Eastern China the Pagoda is surrounded by a Chinese garden. This project was financed by a donation from Wing Yip and Brothers, well known members of the Birmingham Chinese business community. Also in the middle of Holloway Circus is Hebe (Robert Thomas, 1966), a statue erected to mark the building of the inner ring road and representing the Greek goddess with the power to restore youth and vigour.

Out of Town

There are many further works of art all around Birmingham and new pieces appear at regular intervals. In particular, in Heartlands, on the east side of the City, there is a series of new public art commissions at gateways to this development area.

Birmingham has recently taken significant steps to introduce new art for the public in the city, in a growing awareness that a pleasing city environment is very important in attracting both visitors

*Compassion
(Uli Nimptch, 1963)
is to be found outside
the management
offices of Selly Oak
Hospital.*

*Face to Face
(Ray Smith, 1993)
Waterlinks Boulevard,
Aston.*

*Sleeping Iron Giant
(Ondre Nowakowski, 1992)
Garrison Lane,
Bordesley Green.*

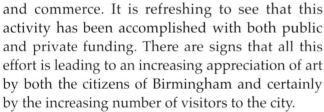

◀

White Curl
(Suzi Gregory, 1993)
outside Waterlinks
House, Aston.

and commerce. It is refreshing to see that this activity has been accomplished with both public and private funding. There are signs that all this effort is leading to an increasing appreciation of art by both the citizens of Birmingham and certainly by the increasing number of visitors to the city.

▶

The Nutcracker performed
by the Birmingham Royal
Ballet (Kevin O'Hare and
Sabrina Lenzi).

Chapter Eight
City of Culture

A ballet company moving to the city and the building of a splendid new concert hall were landmark 1990s events for Birmingham. Symphony Hall has given a tremendous lift to a city with an already strong musical tradition, both by providing a new home for the City of Birmingham Symphony Orchestra and also by attracting the best world orchestras to play in the city. The Birmingham Royal Ballet has prompted an increasing appreciation for ballet and pride in the company.

Music for Hospitals

The Birmingham Triennial Music Festivals of the eighteenth century were an important society event. The first festival was held in 1768 and the triennial festivals began in 1784. Funds from the early concerts were used to help establish the

Firework Fantasia.
The City of Birmingham Symphony Orchestra and fireworks watched by a crowd of 80,000 in Cannon Hill Park in June 1992.

▶

The 150th Anniversary of the performance of Elijah in Birmingham by the Birmingham Festival Choral Society in St Philip's Cathedral.

▼

Birmingham Town Hall.
*The classical design of
Hansom and Welch forms one
side of Victoria Square.
Originally built to house the
Birmingham Triennial Music
Festival, it opened in 1834 but
was not completed until 1850.
Today it awaits renovation so
that it can play a new role in
the life of the city.*

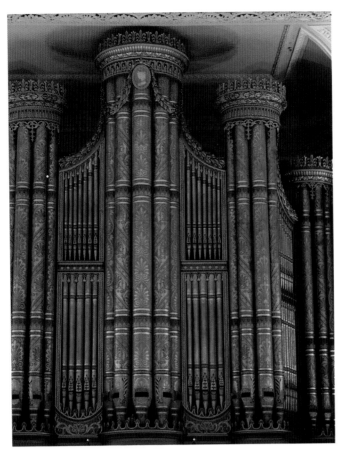

The Town Hall Organ.
This was built by William
Hill in 1850 and many pipes
still have original decoration.

General Hospital, the original purpose for which the festival was conceived. In a history of the festivals Bunce stated that they had 'done so much to make the name of Birmingham famous throughout Europe, as the cultivator and promoter of the musical art in its highest developments'.

By the end of the eighteenth century the Birmingham Triennial Music Festival was established in the national social calendar. Indeed, pick-pockets were reported to travel from London especially for the event.

The attendance of the aristocracy at the festivals, meant that by the end of the eighteenth century nearly £6,000 had been raised towards the work of the General Hospital. In 1834 the Festival was held in the new Town Hall for the first time. The building was not complete but was far enough advanced for the performances which, as always, included *Messiah.* Over the last 160 years, a number of historic musical events have occurred in the Town Hall. Two notable premières were Mendelssohn's *Elijah* in 1846 and Elgar's *The Dream of Gerontius* in 1900.

The Town Hall organ was built by William Hill of London. It has over 4,000 pipes, four sets of keys and nearly eighty stops, with the longest pipe being thirty-five feet. Not surprisingly, it can produce a very wide range of tone and power. Mendelssohn played on the organ and the pipes still retain their original decoration.

City of Birmingham Symphony Orchestra

The City of Birmingham Orchestra was founded in 1920, by public figures such as Neville Chamberlain and the composer Granville Bantock; in 1948 'Symphony' was added to the name. The first symphony concert in the Town Hall was conducted by Sir Edward Elgar. During the 1920s and 1930s the orchestra became established as the major professional Midlands music group, under the direction of Adrian (later Sir Adrian) Boult and Leslie Heward. After the Second World War, George Weldon and Rudolf Schwarz were in command. The international prestige of the CBSO was much increased during the tenure of Hugo Rignold in the 1960s and Louis Frémaux in the 1970s with a number of overseas tours and recordings.

Sakari Oramo, Principal Conductor and Artistic Adviser of the CBSO, is seen with fellow Finnish soloists Lilli Paasikivi and Heikki Kilpelainen after a performance of the Sibelius Kullervo Symphony, Op. 7.

▼

In June 1999 Sir Simon Rattle was appointed as Principal Conductor and Artistic Director of the Berlin Philharmonic Orchestra. Sir Simon takes up the baton of what many regard as the world's finest orchestra in 2002.

In 1980 Simon Rattle became the Principal Conductor and Artistic Adviser to the CBSO and in 1990 its Music Director. Simon Rattle ended eighteen years with the CBSO in style in 1998 with a complete Beethoven symphony cycle. Sir Simon will be remembered for the enormous amount he has done for the resurgence of music in the city. Indeed, Symphony Hall would most probably not exist without him and he has touched everything musical in the city from contemporary music to a renewed interest in Mahler.

The CBSO has its own Symphony Chorus and also plays regularly with the City of Birmingham Choir, both of which are made up of local people. Christopher Robinson has conducted the City of Birmingham Choir since 1964, and such continuity has enabled them to undertake some major choral works in recent times.

Symphony Hall

In 1925 the Principal Conductor, Adrian Boult, was promised a new concert hall; it took until 1991 for this promise to be fulfilled. However, many would say it was worth the wait and the opening of Symphony Hall marked a great achievement for Birmingham. Soon after opening, the hall was being compared to the very best in the world. Symphony Hall has enabled Birmingham to host international orchestras and musicians and to establish international musical associations which would have been impossible without such a venue. It has also played a key role in encouraging young musicians and local groups in the Midlands.

The acoustics of Symphony Hall were designed by the American Russell Johnson of Artec Consultants. The shape of a concert hall is very important and a rectangular 'shoe-box' was chosen in line with classic halls such as the Musikverein in Vienna, the Concertgebouw in Amsterdam and Symphony Hall in Boston. The Birmingham Symphony Hall is constructed of heavy reinforced concrete, with dense surfaces of plaster and stone, which mimic the metre-thick walls of these nineteenth-century halls.

Symphony Hall always aimed to have fine acoustics, but these had to be adaptable to a huge range of events, from the largest orchestra playing the loudest work, to a small ensemble, and from popular music and speech, to conference lectures. A wider range of acoustical character is required for such a variety of events than would normally be found in one room. What makes Symphony Hall so exciting are the design features that enable the acoustics to be altered to give different effects for very different types of performance. Instant changes of this kind are achieved by control of three features: the reverberation chamber, the acoustic curtains and an acoustic canopy. These act to control the type and extent of the 'lateral' sound reflected off surfaces in the hall, rather than the sound coming direct from the source.

A capacity Symphony Hall audience of 2,200 waits to hear Messiah in December 1993.

▼

◄

The City of Birmingham Symphony Orchestra with the CBSO Chorus, the City of Birmingham Choir, children from the School of St Mary and St Anne, Abbots Bromley and Shrewsbury Prep Schools, together with soloists, performing Mahler's Symphony No. 8 (Symphony of a Thousand). Mark Elder was the conductor for this spectacular performance on 5 February 1994.

Sounds Like Birmingham.
Music is fun and in Birmingham there can be a lot of it about!

Top row (left to right)

- *Ronnie Scott, now sadly departed, playing at his club on Broad Street.*
- *Nachda Sansaar.*
- *Cliff Richard sings at the NIA.*

Middle row (left to right)

- *Spirit of the Earth, Chamberlain Square.*
- *The Eureka Jazz Band, Sparkhill Park Fun Day.*

Bottom Row (left to right)

- *The Birmingham Bach Choir in the Adrian Boult Hall.*
- *The Maestros Steel Band.*
- *Jools Holland opens the 1999 Birmingahm International Jazz Festival in The Jam House, St Paul's Square.*
- *Birmingham Group UB40 performing at NEC Arena.*

Widening Musical Appreciation

The Birmingham Early Music Festival and the Birmingham Contemporary Music Group are just two of many examples of musical enterprises that are benefiting from Birmingham's increased musical vitality. The Birmingham Contemporary Music Group was formed in 1987 by players from the CBSO, with Simon Rattle as Artistic Adviser. They quickly became known as a leading contemporary music ensemble and have as a central aim the commissioning and performance of new music.

▲

The Birmingham Early Music Festival stages events at a number of interesting places. Seen here are the Scottish Early Music Consort performing Monteverdi: Scenes of Love and War (The Battle of Tancredi and Clorinda) in the Victorian banking hall of the former Birmingham Town Bank. This now forms part of the offices of Wragge and Co. in Colmore Row.

Ronnie Scott's Jazz Club is on Broad Street and Jools Holland is associated with The Jam House which opened in St Paul's Square in 1999. There are also a number of other pubs and clubs in the city where live music is played all year round.

▶

The Birmingham Contemporary Music Group participated in the British open-air première of Sternklang, by Karlheinz Stockhausen in Cannon Hill Park.

The Tim Amann Quartet playing on a Sunday lunchtime at the Strathallan Hotel, Hagley Road. This weekly session is staged jointly with the hotel, Birmingham Jazz and the Musicians' Union.

Successful City Ballet

In 1989, after several years of informal discussions, Birmingham invited the London-based Sadler's Wells Royal Ballet to consider moving their base to Birmingham and they did so in 1990, making their home in the Hippodrome Theatre in the Chinese Quarter. The origins of the Company date from 1931 when Dame Ninette de Valois founded a company at Sadler's Wells Theatre and it was also associated for many years with the Royal Opera House.

Peter Wright was the Company's Director when it came to Birmingham and in the 1995/96 season David Bintley became the new Artistic Director. Today Birmingham Royal Ballet presents a packed programme in the city and also tours extensively, with a repertoire that includes everything from classical ballet to new works. In 1996 the company

Scenes from the Birmingham Royal Ballet's 1999 production of Coppelia, produced by Peter Wright.

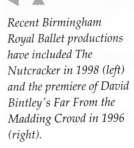

◀ ▲

Recent Birmingham Royal Ballet productions have included The Nutcracker in 1998 (left) and the premiere of David Bintley's Far From the Madding Crowd in 1996 (right).

presented the premiere of David Bintley's *Far from the Madding Crowd* to critical acclaim and every Christmas tickets for *The Nutcracker* are much sought after. The move to Birmingham has been a considerable success both for the ballet company and for the city.

Maturing Cultural Reputation

Birmingham understands the importance of cultural activities in enriching the life of the city and in enhancing its reputation. In the 1990s Symphony Hall has provided a versatile concert hall which has stimulated interest in all forms of music. The establishment of Birmingham Royal Ballet, with an exciting future ahead of it, has significantly added to the city's cultural reputation.

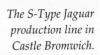

The S-Type Jaguar production line in Castle Bromwich.

Chapter Nine

Industry and Commerce

Towards the end of the nineteenth century the population of Birmingham was approaching 250,000 and the town expanding fast. The great industrial diversity of the city was still mainly based on traditional metal-working and engineering skills. Birmingham dominated the world market in areas such as 'toys', pen-nib manufacture, brass products of all descriptions and a wide variety of other household goods. Industry still relied largely on small workshops but this was soon to change as other countries started to compete in many of Birmingham's traditional markets.

With the coming of the twentieth century increasing mechanisation often required fewer skilled workers and payment changed from piece pay to pay by the hour. At the same time, smaller firms amalgamated to form larger concerns to gain a commercial advantage by economy of scale. New industries included bicycle production and their components and later motorcycles and, of course, cars. There were also many manufacturers producing bicycle components - for example Joseph Lucas,

Brooks saddles are manufactured in Smethwick.

a Birmingham lamp-maker with his 'King of the Road' lamp. By 1911, there were approaching 10,000 people in Birmingham employed in bicycle manufacturing.

Decals are added to frames at Dawes Cycles in Tyseley.

The First and Second World Wars were periods of major industrial activity in the city. Before 1914 the BSA company was making 135 rifles a week but during the First World War this rose to 10,000.

Today bicycle production continues in Birmingham with Dawes in Tyseley making a full range of cycles. Brooks saddles, a divison of Sturmey Archer, still produce traditional leather cycle saddles in Smethwick and these are exported to places such as Holland and Germany. Once worn in, a Brooks saddle is renowned for a comfortable ride.

The original Lucas works in Newtown is marked with a granite memorial.

Motor-car City

Birmingham has a wealth of automobile engineering expertise. On several occasions, the city has introduced radical thinking into car design, which has been influential on a world scale.

At the end of the nineteenth century the manufacture of motor-cars was becoming important in Birmingham and the Austin factory at Longbridge is an excellent example of this development. Herbert Austin built his first car in 1895, while employed at the Wolseley Sheep Shearing Machine Company. Austin's first four-wheel car was the Wolseley Voiturette and this single-cylinder, five-horsepower car won a public trial over 1,000 miles in 1900. In 1905, the Austin Motor Company was formed and Herbert Austin bought the site of a disused printing works at Longbridge close to the Lickey Hills. The company's first car was

Austin Seven cars return to Longbridge each summer.
▼

produced in 1906 and by 1914, 2,000 workers were employed at the factory, producing 1500 cars per year.

In 1921, because of post-war financial difficulties, the Austin Motor Company went into receivership but, using his private resources, Austin secretly developed the Austin Seven at his home Lickey Grange with his assistant, the seventeen-year-old designer Stanley Edge. For eight months, the two men set about designing a low-cost mass-produced car to realise Austin's ambition to 'motorise the masses'. Production started in 1922

Lanchester cars returned to the city to celebrate the 100th anniversary of the first Lanchester, built by the innovative Fred Lanchester in 1895.

Lord Austin's study: Lickey Grange has now been converted to luxury homes.

and the Austin Seven initially cost £225. Between 1922 and the beginning of the Second World War approximately 300,000 Austin Sevens were produced and the Seven was also manufactured under licence in various parts of the world. Indeed the Austin Seven design was the first car that BMW produced.

In the 1950s a second great design change emanated from Longbridge. Alex Issigonis led a team looking at the small car market with a brief to produce an economical car, capable of carrying four people in reasonable comfort. The result was the Mini, launched in 1960, whose radical design featured a space-saving transverse-mounted engine, and front-wheel drive, now standard elements of modern car design.

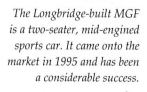

The Longbridge-built MGF is a two-seater, mid-engined sports car. It came onto the market in 1995 and has been a considerable success.

▶

Since developing the Mini, the Birmingham automotive industry has undergone many changes. The Austin name was finally lost in 1989, when British Aerospace took over the company with the formation of their Rover car division and this was sold to BMW on 31 January 1994. The Longbridge factory, now called Rover Birmingham, is subject to major investment plans by BMW, Birmingham City Council and the British Government.

In Solihull the Land Rover factory produces four-wheel-drive cars such as the Range Rover, Discovery, Defender and Freelander. The original Land Rover was launched at the Amsterdam Motor Show in 1948; it cost £450 and, to start with, doors came as an optional extra. Since then over 1.5 million Land Rovers have been sold.

The Range Rover, Discovery and Land Rover Defender are all produced at the Solihull factory.

The Freelander: This car was involved in a trip to visit 50 countries in as many days.

The Rover 75 was launched at the 1998 Motor Show in Birmingham.

Jaguar S-Type Reborn

A success story is unfolding in Heartlands as Jaguar starts a concerted effort to enter the more affordable end of the quality car market, with 50 percent of total Jaguar production now taking place in Castle Bromwich. The Jaguar body assembly and paint shop at Castle Bromwich produces the bodies for the Jaguar XJ and XK range which are then assembled at the Browns Lane plant in Coventry. At Castle Bromwich £200 million has been invested in a brand new plant for the manufacture of the S-Type Jaguar, the company's first compact luxury saloon since the 1960s.

LDV continues to find a market niche, producing vans and minibuses at their Washwood Heath factory in Heartlands.

The Jensen S-V8 was launched at the 1998 British International Motor Show at the NEC and manufacturing starts in 2000. In true Jensen style the car has a high performance version of the V8, 4.6 litre Ford Cobra engine.

▶

The Jaguar XK8 together with the C-Type in which Stirling Moss won the Mille Miglia in 1954 and an SS100 at Castle Bromwich Hall.

▼

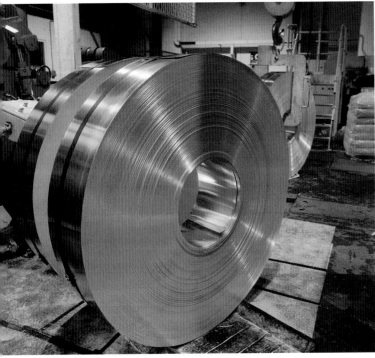

Production of non-ferrous strip at B Mason uses processes including continuous casting, cold rolling and slitting.

Key to Success in Aston

A notable example of the surviving Birmingham brass industry is the firm B Mason and Sons Ltd, who manufacture specialist copper alloys at their premises at Wharf Street in Aston. Started by Ben Mason in 1852 close to the present premises, the company manufactures non-ferrous strip using continuous casting followed by cold rolling and slitting. Mason products are used in the lock, door furniture and lighting industries and phosphor bronze is made for the electrical connector industry.

Mason also produces 'key metal', a leaded nickel-silver alloy, and the company is the main world-wide producer. Leaded nickel-silver has the superior milling qualities needed for key production but 'key metal' is not an easy alloy to cast and the precise composition and casting conditions are not discussed with visiting photographers!

In 1988 B Mason Ltd became part of the German Wieland-Werke AG group of companies. As a supplier of raw material for other industries, the Birmingham operation has ensured continued growth and success by marketing its products around the world. Mason currently employs 150 people and is undergoing a sizeable investment programme, including expansion at their facilities by the canal close to the Aston clock.

Balancing Goes Hi-Tech

Historically the Birmingham manufacturing environment encourages those with good ideas, determination and the sheer hard work to succeed. The firm BTD is a modern-day example, designing and producing specialist balancing machines at their premises at Garrett's Green close to Birmingham Airport. The company has an innovative approach to industrial balancing with their computerised control systems enabling cost-effective process control and automation.

Like many good ideas BTD started in a Birmingham garage. Today their equipment and

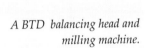

Staff at BTD with a computer-controlled balancing machine destined for the automotive industry.

A BTD balancing head and milling machine.

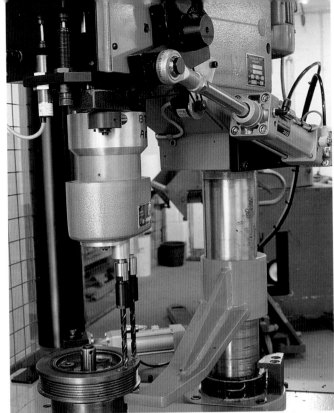

expertise are exported around the world and success springs from the ability to drive innovative ideas forward faster than less dynamic competitors. Indeed, one source of BTD work is refurbishing competitors' machines, sending them back to work with a BTD computer controller installed.

Underground in Heartlands

There are large-scale industrial operations carried on in Birmingham of which many city-dwellers are unaware. This is certainly the case at Washwood Heath in Heartlands where Alstom produce everything from London underground trains to high-speed trains.

Trains have been manufactured at Washwood Heath since 1843 and 1,300 people are employed on site at present. Investment in public transport is leading to major contracts for Alstom and high-profile projects include the Gatwick Express and suburban trains for operators all over the country. Of great interest to long-suffering Birmingham travellers is the Virgin Rail contract for a fleet of 54

Alstom at Washwood Heath is a modern plant making trains for a wide variety of customers including London Transport.

eight-car, tilting, high-speed trains which will bring much needed improvements to the service between Birmingham and London Euston in the twenty-first century.

Hi-Tech on the Banks of the River Cole

Specialist Computer Holdings (SCH) demonstrates that Birmingham can succeed in new technology and that the traditional Birmingham entrepreneurial approach continues. SCH specialises in strategic information technology partnerships with major corporate and public sector clients.

Peter Rigby, who founded and runs SCH, first gained experience with American computer companies before investing his savings in 1976 to set up his computer business. SCH's headquarters are in Tyseley beside the River Cole. The company employs over 2,000 staff and turns over £600 million a year. In 1999 SCH will deliver over 300,000 PCs and a million computer-related products. The company stresses the value of investment and has recently opened a new commissioning complex. Predicting client needs and concentrating on offering comprehensive support have brought success to SCH.

Below: The River Cole in Tyseley offers a very different view of Specialist Computer Holdings.
Bottom left: The SCH commissioning plant where PCs are configured for clients.
Bottom Right: Hi-Tech stock control at SCH.

Cadbury World gives an excellent introduction to chocolate-making at the Bournville factory. Seen here is a replica of the Bull Street shop opened by John Cadbury in 1824. The tour of Cadbury World includes demonstrations of hand-made chocolate production.

'Farm', Sparkbrook, dating from the mid-18th century, was the home of the original Lloyd's Bank family.
The house survived the Priestley Riots of 1791 and is an excellent example of Birmingham architecture of the period.

◀

Birmingham Banks and Commerce

Since the eighteenth century, industrial activity in Birmingham has required substantial financing which led to the establishment of a number of banks in the city, the best known today being Lloyds TSB and the Midland Bank (now known as HSBC). Before the advent of commercial banks, it was the practice for merchants to lend money to manufacturers to buy raw materials and pay their workers' wages.

New industries were sometimes started when profits from another area of work were re-invested in new projects. Josiah Mason used his fortune made from split-ring production to start large-scale pen manufacturing, and the printing business of John Baskerville was sustained on the profits from his japanning business.

City 2000, the financial services promotional organisation, works with the City Council, Birmingham Marketing Partnership and Birmingham Chamber of Commerce and Industry to promote the city. Birmingham is a regional centre, and this is reflected in the major corporate names in

Prestige office buildings on Colmore Row as seen from the cupola of St Philip's Cathedral with the Telecom Tower behind.

▼

159

banking, insurance, accountancy and other professions who have offices in the city. 'Locate in Birmingham' is an important partnership between Birmingham City Council Economic Development Department and others, charged with assisting relocation and expansion projects in Birmingham.

Today the infrastructure of the commercial district of Birmingham is undergoing regeneration. Modern office premises are being produced, both by the refurbishment of existing buildings and the construction of brand new ones. In the city centre, Colmore Row is a fine example of what can be done by making use of Victorian buildings and upgrading them for modern office use. At the Snow Hill end of Colmore Row is a group of modern office buildings, with Colmore Gate and The Wesleyan certainly being eye-catching. Close by, the former Lewis's department store has been converted to a large office development.

Colmore Circus is a meeting place for modern high-rise office blocks.

Exhibitions and Conventions

In the 1970s it was decided to build the National Exhibition Centre, (NEC), to the east of the city, at Bickenhill, next to Birmingham Airport. The first phase was opened in 1976 and the centre has been a continuing success; with further development of the site ensuring that the NEC is a leading venue for exhibitions of all descriptions, including the British Motor Show. The NEC Arena has also been very successful at staging large musical events.

Building on the experience of the NEC and faced with a declining industrial base, Birmingham decided to extend the NEC concept with a convention centre of international standing, right in the heart of Birmingham. The site chosen was that of the old Bingley Hall, on Broad Street, which had been erected in 1850, and was an innovative exhibition hall in its time, capable of holding 20,000 people. Construction of the International Convention Centre (ICC) began in 1986, opening for business on 2 April 1991. The ICC is used for meetings and exhibitions of all descriptions, from a small group of half a dozen, to a large congress with associated exhibitions and many thousands of delegates. Marketing a conference venue is a long-term business; international congresses are often booked many years in advance and

▲

Birmingham International Airport is at Bickenhill, just a 10-minute rail ride from the centre of the city. The NEC opened in 1976 and has been expanding ever since. Besides being a major centre for exhibitions and conferences the NEC also stages large pop concerts.

Crufts is another national event that has found a home at the NEC.

An exhibition of medical equipment at the NIA shows just how versatile this venue can be.

◀

Birmingham has done well to attract a significant number of world congresses.

Financing Change

The economy of Birmingham is still changing, from a predominantly industrialised manufacturing centre, to a much more mixed economy. Although innovations such as the NEC and ICC may be considered part of the service sector, they are also helpful in giving prestige and back-up to the city, which should encourage inward investment in the manufacturing sectors and thus further strengthen the local economy. Birmingham's engineering expertise is a very valuable resource. Despite the difficult economic climate of the 1980s and the loss of many manufacturing jobs, engineering expertise must surely form an important part of the continuing renewal of Birmingham into the twenty-first century.

▶

Phoenix Village Hall in Bordesley Village is run by Bournville Village Trust.

Staff from Birmingham Children's Hospital at their new home in Steelhouse Lane.

Jalebi manufacture at the Vaisakhi Sikh Festival in Handsworth Park.

The Birmingham to Oxford bike ride leaves the NEC.

Chapter Ten
Life in the City

Birmingham is a green city, full of tree-lined roads, parks and other open spaces and there is a great deal to see and do. This book is no more than a personal glimpse of Birmingham, its history, people and ways of life, through images of the present-day city.

The Lickey Hills are a popular area for relaxation with panoramic views of the city.

▶

University Life

There are three Universities in the city: Birmingham University, at Edgbaston, Aston University with its campus close to the city centre and the University of Central England (UCE) based at Perry Barr, but with departments in various parts of the city. The total student population reading for degrees at the three universities is now over 30,000 and is expected to rise over the next few years.

'Old Joe' is named after Joseph Chamberlain and is a dominant feature in the centre of Birmingham University.

▼

Fun on the Streets

There are many organised public events in Birmingham each year, probably the biggest and

most colourful is Birmingham Carnival which first came to the city in 1983. For an entire weekend the city reverberates to the sound of music and the carnival parade itself is mainly on foot in true Caribbean style with a great feeling of fun.

The Birmingham Carnival.

Birmingham for a New Beginning

Immigration has always been important to Birmingham's growth and development. Even some of the Welsh stonemasons, who brought the Anglesey marble to build the Town Hall in the 1830s, decided to settle in the town. Higher wages drew workers into Birmingham from the surrounding agricultural areas and between 1801 and 1831 the population of Birmingham nearly doubled.

The most recent figures, from the 1991 census for the make-up of the Birmingham population, defined by ethnic groups are:

Ethnic Origin	No. of People	%
White	754,274	78.5
Pakistani	66,085	6.9
Indian	51,075	5.3
Black Caribbean	44,770	4.7
Bangladeshi	12,739	1.3
Black Other	11,606	1.2
Other (non-white)	20,492	2.1
Total	**961,041**	**100%**

During the twentieth century Birmingham has been a natural centre to come and settle in, offering comparatively good employment opportunities in both the manufacturing and service sectors, as well as opportunities to start new businesses. It has the largest ethnic minority population in a British city with around 25 per cent of the city's nearly one million inhabitants being of non-white origin, compared with a national average of about

The Sikh funeral procession of Bhai Sahib Norang Singh Ji moves along the Soho Road in Handsworth.

▶

Birmingham Hippodrome, the home of the Birmingham Royal Ballet, is in the middle of the Chinese Quarter with many popular Chinese restaurants all around.

◀

5 per cent. Such a wide range of cultural backgrounds adds new dimensions to the city's life. Indeed, Birmingham has worked hard to ensure that people understand and appreciate the different cultures that surround them.

Interestingly, the Birmingham Chinese population is just 0.3 per cent of the total but has a high profile. A Chinese Quarter close to the Hippodrome contains many Chinese businesses including restaurants and suppliers to the Chinese catering trade. Indeed, the cultural diversity of Birmingham has led to a wide range of food to enjoy when eating out. Of all the tastes to be found, the most celebrated is surely the Balti Curry.

Chinese New-Year celebrations at the Arcadian Centre in the Birmingham Chinese Quarter.

Going for a Balti

A Balti is literally a metal dish with two handles, similar to a small wok, in which a Balti Curry should be cooked and served. In Birmingham this type of cooking originates mainly from the Sparkbrook and Sparkhill areas of the inner city but is now found all over Birmingham. Many of the original Balti Houses were established along Stoney Lane, Ladypool Road and the Stratford

Balti House Cuisine.
From raw ingredients to
finished product.
▶

170

Birmingham Central Mosque is a landmark on the middle ring road. Birmingham University tower can be seen in the distance. ▶

Road just to the south of the city centre. A traditional Balti House or Sweet Centre has Asian sweets in the window and a simple restaurant area behind. A Balti is usually eaten with naan bread, used to scoop up the curry, and almost never with rice. Balti cooking is thought to have its origins in the Indian North-West Frontier and to have spread from there to the Kashmir and Punjab regions. Spices such as coriander, cardamom, ginger, fennel and cumin are all basic ingredients. Original Balti cooking produced a dry dish, but the Birmingham version has been 'Westernised' by the addition of a sauce.

The success of the Balti is surely due to a combination of several factors. Balti cooking can be very pleasant on the taste-buds, the atmosphere of a Balti House is very relaxing and eating out Balti-style can be extremely cheap.

A Different View of Birmingham

Birmingham first installed closed circuit television in the city centre in 1989. Citywatch, an organisation with input from Birmingham City Council, West Midlands Police and private organisations, oversees the project. The control room is at Steelhouse Lane police station and is operational 24 hours a day. In 1998 the system was upgraded

partly because of the G8 Summit and there are now 36 city-centre cameras with plans for many more.

Eight cameras are mounted on stainless steel beacons, a new item of street furniture designed by Birmingham City Council and providing a better camera position than wall-mounted cameras. Continuous CCTV recordings produce six video-tapes each day and private surveillance tapes from around the city are also used to help with investigations if a major incident occurs. Operators can be surprised at how oblivious some people are to the presence of city-centre cameras.

One of the CCTV Beacons in Birmingham city centre.
▼

Looking Down on the City

The West Midlands Police helicopter has become a familiar sight over Birmingham for over ten years. It operates from its base at the Elmdon Building at Birmingham Airport, flying approximately 3,000 operations a year. The unit includes twelve police observers and five pilots, together with two civilian support staff and provides 24-hour support. It plays an important role in policing major public events and figures of arrests and recovery of stolen property are impressive. Onboard equipment includes camera, thermal imager, searchlight and various devices for surveillance and tracking. However it is reassuring that a well-thumbed copy of the Birmingham A to Z is also an important piece of equipment.

Improving Public Transport

The AS355 F2 Squirrel police helicopter outside the old Elmdon Airport terminal building. A new helicopter, an MD 902 Explorer, will soon be in service.

A member of the West Midlands Police Air Operations Unit.

A new public transport strategy unveiled in 1999 emphasises an integrated public transport system. Buses are seen as the major form of public transport with clean, high frequency buses in a distinctive livery. The transport strategy considers the use of other forms of rapid transport including further development of Midland Metro.

Midland Metro Line One finally opened to passengers in June 1999. The 20 km route runs from Snow Hill station in Birmingham to Wolverhampton. It uses the old Great Western Railway line through Handsworth and the Black Country towns of West Bromwich, Wednesbury and Bilston and goes onto the road at Monmore Green for the last leg into Wolverhampton. Trams run every six minutes in peak periods with a journey time for the whole route of thirty-five minutes.

Midland Metro accelerates through West Bromwich Central.

▶

Midland Metro at Snow Hill Station with Colmore Circus in the background.

▼

First Class Football and Cricket

There are three major football teams in the City. Aston Villa have their ground at Villa Park, built on part of the original Aston Hall grounds. Birmingham City is based at St Andrew's, set on high ground to the east of the City and West Bromwich Albion's ground is based at the Hawthorns just across the city border in Sandwell. Changes in ground safety regulations in the 1990s mean that all three grounds now have fine all-seater stadiums.

Edgbaston is the home of Warwickshire Cricket Club and is also a regular venue for test matches. The ground was established on the banks of the River Rea, where cricket has been played since the first major match against the MCC in June 1886.

International Sporting Events

The National Indoor Arena and National Exhibition Centre provide venues for important sporting events.

In 1999 the NIA hosted Davis Cup tennis during the celebrations of 100 years of this event. Tension and excitement mounted as Tim Henman and

Warwickshire cricket ground with Cannon Hill Park in the foreground.

Birmingham City, known as 'The Blues' play at St Andrew's.

The NIA was packed for the Great Britain versus USA Davis Cup match in 1999. Lawn tennis originated in Edgbaston where it was first played in 1865.

Greg Rusedski battled against the American team in a world group tie. This event was a landmark for tennis with a quite different style of support from the capacity NIA crowd over all three days. The fabulous atmosphere created in the arena will live for a long time in the minds of those who were present and the millions who watched on television.

Besides sporting events the NIA also hosts large-scale entertainment events ranging from grand operatic productions to ice spectaculars.

Sport for All

For those who wish to take part in sport rather than just watch, Birmingham has excellent facilities. There are numerous well-used sports centres throughout the city, a number of municipal golf courses that don't require membership and sailing clubs on a number of reservoirs. Sutton Park is an amazing resource where all these activities are available and one can even join the model aeroplane club or spend the day walking this great expanse of open space.

Positively Birmingham

Birmingham's people have always thrived on change. In the twelfth century they created a bustling market town. The eighteenth century saw a huge surge in industrial activity. In the nineteenth century the city led the way in the drive for decent living conditions. Twentieth-century Birmingham has been an industrial world leader.

▲

Sport for all:
Moseley Rugby Club
play at 'The Reddings'
in Moseley.

The Birmingham Bullets
basketball team play at
the National Indoor
Arena.

Solihull Blaze ice hockey
team have a dedicated
following.

Sailboarding at
Bartley Green .

▶

The Birmingham Wheels
Project in Bordesley.

▼

Birmingham Botanical Gardens are fun for children too.

Today, Birmingham's people face another period of change; large in scale but harder to define. Fine new buildings and contemporary art go hand in hand with the re-discovery and regeneration of architectural heritage and industrial tradition, to create an exciting, prosperous and thriving city.

Above all else Birmingham has succeeded because of the skills, enterprise and positive attitude of the people who have chosen to live in the city. This positive attitude is the key to the Third Millennium.

Bibliography

The following will be of interest if you would like to read in more depth or are researching aspects of Birmingham.

Briggs, Asa, *History of Birmingham* vol II, Oxford University Press, 1952

Cherry, Gordan, *Birmingham: A Study in Geography, History and Planning*, John Wiley, Chichester, 1994.

Chinn, Carl, *Birmingham: The Great Working City*, Birmingham City Council, 1994.

Church, Roy, *Herbert Austin: The British Motor Car Industry to 1941*, Europa Publications, London, 1979.

Dent, Robert, *Old and New Birmingham*, Houghton & Hammond, Birmingham, 1880.

Dent, Robert, *The Making of Birmingham*. J.L. Allday, Birmingham, 1894.

Fairclough, Oliver, *The Grand Old Mansion: The Holtes and Their Successors at Aston Hall 1618-1864*, Birmingham Museums and Art Gallery, 1984.

Foster, Richard, *Birmingham New Street; Background and Beginnings*, Chapter 2 'Birmingham's Canals', Wild Swan Publications, Didcot, 1990.

Gerard, AJ and Slater, TR (eds.), *Managing a Conurbation; Birmingham and its Region*, K.A.F. Brewin Books, Studley, 1996.

Gill, Conrad, *History of Birmingham* vol I, Oxford University Press, 1952.

Gledhill, Alison, *Birmingham's Jewellery Quarter*, K.A.F. Brewin Books, Studley, Warwickshire, 1988.

Haddleton, Marie, *The Jewellery Quarter: History and Guide*, YBA Publications, Birmingham, 1987.

Holyoak, Joe, *All About Victoria Square*, The Victorian Society, Birmingham Branch, 1989.

Hutton, William, *An History of Birmingham*, 2nd (1783) and 3rd (1795) Editions, Thomas Pearson, Birmingham, (2nd edition reprinted by EP Publishing in 1976).

Little, Bryan, *Birmingham Buildings: The Architectural Story of a Midland City*, David & Charles, Newton Abbot, 1971.

Pearson, J.M., *Canal Companion: Birmingham Canal Navigations*, J.M. Pearson and Associates, Burton-on-Trent, Staffs, 1989.

Pugh, Bridget and Crews, Anne, *Solid Citizens: Statues in Birmingham*, Westwood Press Publications, Sutton Coldfield, 1983.

Sidey, Tessa, *Public Art in Birmingham*, Birmingham Museums and Art Gallery, 1993.

Skipp, Victor, *A History of Greater Birmingham Down to 1830*, Victor Skipp, Yardley, Birmingham, 1980.

Skipp, Victor, *The Making of Victorian Birmingham*, Victor Skipp, Yardley, Birmingham, 1983.

Stephens, W.B. (ed.), *The Victoria History of the Counties of England*. vol VII: *The City of Birmingham*, Oxford University Press, 1964.

Sutcliffe, Anthony, and Smith, Roger, *History of Birmingham* vol III: *Birmingham 1939 - 1970*, Oxford University Press, 1974.

Tilson, Barbara (ed.), *Made in Birmingham: Design and Industry 1889 - 1989*, K.A.F. Brewin Books, Studley, Warwickshire, 1989.

Upton, Chris, *A History of Birmingham*, Phillimore & Co., Chichester, 1993.

Index

A bold page number indicates a photograph

All that Glisters **80**
Alstom 154-6, **155**
Angel of the North 8
Antley, Lyn **76**
Apha Tower 92
Archer, Thomas 27, 30
Arena Central 46, 92
Argent Centre **72**
Artec Consultants 134
Assay Office 34, **69**;
    hallmark **69**;
    millennium hallmark **76**
Associated Architects 76
Aston Hall 23-27, **23-26**
Aston Hall and Park
    Company 26
Aston Park 2
Aston Villa F.C 176
Attwood, Thomas **119**
Austin Seven **146**, 147-8
Austin, Lord Herbert 146

Balti Curry 169-71, **170**
banks 159
Bartley Green Reservoir **179**
Baskerville, John 115, 159
Beacon, CCTV **172**
Beleschenko, Alexander 116
Bermingham, Peter de 16
Bickenhill 161
Big Peg **67,** 76
Bintley, David 141-2
Birdlife **107,** 116, **117**
Birmingham Alliance 99, 101
Birmingham and Fazeley
    Canal 52, 95
Birmingham Bach Choir **138**
Birmingham Bullets **178**
Birmingham Canal Navigation
    Company (BCN) 48, 54
Birmingham Carnival **166**
Birmingham Chamber of
    Commerce and Industry 159
Birmingham City Council 12,
    149, 159, 160
Birmingham City F.C. **176**
Birmingham Contemporary
    Music Group **140**
Birmingham Early Music
    Festival **140**

Birmingham Festival Choral
    Society **128**
Birmingham International
    Airport 153 **161**;
    Elmdon Building **173**
Birmingham International
    Motor Show **150, 151,** 161
Birmingham Marketing
    Partnership 159
Birmingham Mint **70,** 70-1
Birmingham Museums and
    Art Gallery 35
Birmingham Railway
    Museum **58-9**
Birmingham Royal
    Ballet **127, 141-2**
Birmingham School of Art 112
Birmingham Small Arms
    (BSA) 82, 145
Birmingham Triennial Music
    Festival 128, 132
Birmingham University **164**;
    Field Archeology Unit **16**
Birmingham Wheels **178**
Black Country 16, 19, 48, 54, 173
Blair, Tony & Cherie **11**
Blakesley Hall 21, **22**
Bloye, William 32, 112
BMW 149
Bond, The **49**
Bordesley Village **61, 163**
Boult, Sir Adrian 133; Hall **138**
Boulton Watt and Sons 38
Boulton, Matthew 32, 70
Boulton, Matthew Robinson 23
*Boulton, Watt & Murdock
    Statue* 32, **112**
Bournville Village Trust 162
brass industry 153
Bright, John 86
Brindley, James 48; pub **52**
Brindleyplace **92**
Brindleyplace Bar **92**
*Britannia Rewarding the
    Manufacturers of
    Birmingham* 2, **5**
British Metal Treatments **106**
Broad Street 92, 161
Broadway Plaza, site **94**
Brooks saddles **144**
BTD 153-4, **154**
Budd, Kenneth 95, 121
Bull Ring 99-101; **100;**
    new (model) 101
Bunce 132

Burne-Jones windows **27**
Cadbury World **157**

canals 45-64;
    fibre-optic cable 62;
    living **60,** 60-1;
    renovation 46, 60, 64
Canon Hill Park **129**
Castle Bromwich 150; Hall **151**
Centenary Square **107, 109,
    110-1, 113-5**
Central Mosque **171**
Chamberlain Clock **67**
Chamberlain Memorial
    Fountain 117, **118**
Chamberlain Square 117-19, **118**
Chamberlain, Joseph 2, 84, 86
Chantrey, Francis 40, 42
Chartist Movement 6
Chartist Riots 6, 119
Children's Hospital **94, 163**
Chinese Quarter 141, **168**
City 2000 159
city centre skyline **iv, 18**
City Heights 95, **96**
City Hospital 57
City of Birmingham
    Choir 134, **136-7**
City of Birmingham Symphony
    Orchestra **128-37**
Civic Gospel 86
Clayton, Lisa 6
Clinton, Bill **10**
Closed Circuit Television
    (CCTV) 171-2;
    control room **172**
coat of arms **87,** 112
Colmore Circus **160**
Colmore family 66, 71
Colmore Row **159,** 160
Commerce 159-62
Compassion **125**
Construction: An Allegory **116**
Cooper, John **148**
Coppelia **141**
Coppinger, Sioban 119
Cornish tin mines 36-8
Corporation Street 88, 120
Council House **1,** 2
Crufts **161**
Curzon Street Railway
    Bridge 48,
Curzon Street Station **102**
Custard Factory **105**
cycling **62, 163**

Davis Cup 176-7, **177**
Dawes Cycles **145**
Dawson, George **86**
Digbeth Canal Basin 81
Digbeth Millennium
    Quarter 104-6
Discovery Centre 103
Domesday Book 16
Dream of Gerontius 133

Edgbaston Reservoir **55**
Edge 5
Eginton, Francis 71, 72,
Elder, Mark 137
Elijah **128**
ethnic mix 167
Eureka Jazz Band **138**
Eykyn, Roger 71

Face to Face **124**
Far from the Madding Crowd **142**
Fellows Morton & Clayton 48
Firework Fantasia **129**
Focus Foyer 95, **96, 98**
football 176
Forward 8, **107,** 112, **113**

G8 Summit 10-13, 94
Galton Bridge **48**
Garrett's Green 153
Gas Street Basin 48, **50-51**
General Hospital 132
Gormley, Antony 8
Gough, Piers 92
Grammar School,
    The old; Yardley **20;**
    King's Norton **21**
Grand Union canal walk **62**
*Guardians, The Victoria
    Square* **7**, 8
Guillotine Lock **47,** 54
Gun Barrel Proof House **57,** 81
Gun Quarter 81
gunmaking **82**

Hall of Memory 109
Hancock, Tony 120; statue **121**
Handsworth, Sikh funeral
    procession **167**
Hansom, Joseph 5, 130
Haselden, Ron 106
Head Post Office, former 2, **4**
Heartlands **61, 124,** 150, 154
Heaton, Ralph 71
Hebe **123**
Highbury **88**
Hill, William 133
Hippodrome, Birmingham **169**
Hockley Brook 33

Hockley Port **60,** 61
Holloway Circus **122**
Holte family 23
Hub, The 103

Ikon Gallery **83**
immigration 166-8
Improvement Scheme 88
Industry and Genius 115-16, **115**
International Convention
    Centre (ICC) 12, **45,** 107, 161;
    public art in **116-17**
International Lions **14**
Iron Man 8, **9**
Issigonis, Alex 148

Jaguar S-Type 150;
    production line **143**
Jaguar XK8, C-Type, SS100 **151**
Jalebi manufacture **163**
Jam House, The **139,** 140
James I 23
Jaray, Tess 109
Jenkins, William 91
Jensen S-V8 **151**
Jewellery Quarter 65-81
Jewellery Quarter Business
    Centre **65,** 74
Johnson, Russell 134
Jones, Mick **68**
Jubilee 2000 10-11, **11**

Kaufman, Pat 80
Kennedy Memorial **95,** 121
King's Norton **21-2**

Ladypool Junior and Infant
    School **89**
Lanchester cars **147**
Land Rover cars **149**
Lapthorne, Lee 80
LDV **150**
Leather working 16
Legge Lane **78**
Leland, John 19
Levitt Bernstein Associates 82
Lewis's department store **120**
Lickey Grange, study **147**
Lickey Hills 146, **165**
Lloyds TSB Bank 159
Lloyd's Farm **158**
Lomax, Tom 109, 112, 114
London Underground tube
    trains 154-6, **155**
Longbridge 146-9
Lord Roberts of Kandahar 91
Lucas, Joseph 145

Lunar Society 42-4;
    Room **43**

Maestros Steel Band **138**
Mailbox 92
Mamod **39**
markets **17**
Martin and Chamberlain 87, 89
Martineau Galleries 101
Mason, B **152,** 153
Mason, Josiah 159
Mason, Raymond 106, 112
Masshouse 101, **104**
Mendelssohn 133
Messiah 133, 135
Metchley Camp 16
MGF **148**
Midland Bank (HSBC) 159
Midland Metro 8, 173, **174-5**
Millennium Point 36, 101-4, **101**
Mini 148 ; Cooper **148**
Minton tiles **84**
Mistry, Dhruva 7-8
Moseley Rugby Club **178**
motor-car manufacture 146-51
Municipal Revolution 14
Murdock, William 36-8;
    cottage **38,**
    steam carriage **39**
Museum of the Jewellery
    Quarter **68,** 77

National Exhibition Centre
    (NEC) 12, 161
National Indoor Arena **162**
National Sealife Centre **64**
Nelson Statue **108**
Nettlefold J.S. 84, 86
New Year Fireworks **63,**
    first in Centenary
    Square **110-11**
Number 1 Victoria Square 5
Number Three Brindleyplace **93**
Nutcracker, The **127, 142**

O'Hare, Kevin **127**
Old Crown, The **19**
Old Joe **164**
Old Square 119-21, **120**
Old Turn Junction **54,** 63
Oozells Square **83**
Oozells Street School **83, 89**
Oramo, Sakari **133**
Oriental Pagoda **122**

Parcels Office, Old 5
Parry, F.C. **35**
Patten, David 115
pen nib industry **74**

per cent for art 109
Petherbridge, Deanna 116
Phoenix Village Hall **163**
Porphyrios Associates 92
Potter, Marge **10**
Priestley Riots 44
Priestley, Joseph 44; statue **42**
Prince of Wales 64, 78
Princess Diana **6**, 30
pub architecture, Victorian **91**
public art **107-126**
public transport 173-5
Pugin A.W.N. 84

Queen Elizabeth II Law
    Courts 40
Queen Victoria 2, **6**, 26-7

railways 55-6
Rattle, Sir Simon **134**, 140
Red Lion, Handsworth **91**
Richard, Sir Cliff **139**
Rigby, Peter 156
River Cole **156**
River Rea 16, **104**, 176
River Tame 16
River, The **3**, **8**
Roberts, James 99
Robinson, Christopher 134
Roman remains 16
Ronnie Scott's Jazz Club 138, 140
Rotunda **57**, **99**
'Rover 75' **150**
Rowland, Peter **82**

St Chad's Cathedral 81, **84**,
    85, **97**
St Chad's Circus **95-98**
St Martin's Church 99, **100**
St Mary's Church,
    Handsworth **40**
St Nicholas's Church, Kings's
    Norton **15**, **22**
St Paul's Church 71, **73**
St Philip's Cathedral
    27-30, **28-9**, **30**, **128**
Salviati 2
Sansaar, Nachda **139**
Sarehole Mill **33**, **34**
School of Jewellery **75**, 76
Scott, Ronnie **138**
Secombe, Harry **121**
Sherborne Wharf **60**
Sleeping Iron Giant **124**
Smethwick Engine **37**, 103
Smith and Pepper 77
Snow Hill Station 95, **174**
Soho Foundry 36
Soho House **31**, 34-5, **43**

Soho Loop **57**
Soho Manufactory 33-5
Soho Pool 33
Solihull Blaze **178**
Spaghetti Junction **56**
Specialist Computer Holdings
    (SCH) **156**
Spirit of Birmingham **6**
Spirit of Enterprise 112-5, **114**
Spirit of the Earth **138**
Spring Hill Library **87**
steam engines 35-39, **37**, **39**
Steelhouse Lane Police
    Station **172**
Stratford Canal 22, 54
Stratford House 19, **20**, 21-2
Sutton Park 16
Symphony Court 60
Symphony Hall 128, 134-7,
    135, 136-7
Symphony Hall Mural **116**

Technology Innovation
    Centre 103
Telford, Thomas 54-5
terracotta 84, 91
Thomas, Robert 123
Thomason, Yeoville 2
Tim Amann Quartet 141
Toft, Albert 109
tourism 77
Town Crier 12
Town Hall 5-6, **130-1**;
    organ **132**
'toy' - making 32, **35**, 66, 71
Triennial Music Festival 128
Tyseley 156

UB40 **139**
universities 164
University of Central England
    (UCE) 76
University of the First Age 103
urban village 78,
    Digbeth 104 ;
    Heartlands **61**, **163**;
    Jewellery Quarter 80

Vaisakhi Sikh festival 163
Victoria Law Courts **90**, 91
Victoria Square **1-14**
Victorian Society 2, 4
Vittoria Street **79**
Vyse Estate 66

Warwick and Birmingham
    Canal 49
Warwick Bar **53**, 54

Warwickshire Cricket
    Ground **176**
Washwood Heath 154
Watt, James 32, 35-6, 40
Watt, James Jnr. 23, 38
Wattilisk **41**, 42
Wednesbury coalfield 48
Welch 5
West Bromwich Albion 176
West Midlands Police
    Helicopter 172, **173**
Westmacott, Richard 108
White Curl **126**
Wieland-Werke 153
Wiley W.E. 72
Wing Yip and Brothers 123
Wolseley Sheep Shearing
    Machine Company 146
Worcester and Birmingham
    Canal **22**, 47
Worcester Bar 53
Wright, Peter 141

Youth 8